It's Not ~~Just~~ About the Money

How to Build Authentic Major Donor Relationships
REVISED and UPDATED Edition

By Richard Perry and Jeff Schreifels

Copyright ©2020 by Richard Perry and Jeff Schreifels.
All rights reserved.

ISBN 9781679890406

This book may not be reproduced, in whole or in part, in any form (beyond that copying permitted by Sections 107 and 108 of the U. S. Copyright Law and except by reviewers for the public press), without written permission from the authors.

www.veritusgroup.com

CONTENTS

Foreword 5

Introduction 9

Part 1: Discovering the Heart of Fundraising

    Chapter 1. Why People Need to Give 13

    Chapter 2. Getting Your Organization Back on Track.... 19

    Chapter 3. Building a Culture of Philanthropy 29

    Pause for Thought: Everyone Needs an Excuse 39

    Chapter 4. Taking Your Donor to the Need............ 41

    Pause for Thought: The Power of Yes—and No 53

    Chapter 5. Pitfalls to Avoid 57

    Pause for Thought: Beware of the Giant Hairball......... 73

    Chapter 6. Setting Up for Success 75

Part 2: Building Your Major Gifts Program

    Chapter 7. The Seven Pillars of Major Gift Strategy..... 99

    Chapter 8. Creating the Perfect Donor Pool 107

    Pause for Thought: The Worst Day of My Career........ 123

    Chapter 9. Creating Effective Donor Offers 127

    Chapter 10. Permission-Based Asking................ 141

    Pause for Thought: A Success Story 177

    Chapter 11. Managing Up 181

    Chapter 12. Closing the Circle: Thank Yous,
Reporting Back, and Accountability 185

    Chapter 13. Heed These Critical Indispensables 193

Closing Thoughts..................................... 213

Acknowledgments 215

About the Authors 217

Foreword

I'll never forget the smell of Happy Teriyaki.

It was while I worked at The Domain Group, the Seattle-based fundraising agency that roared to prominence in the mid-90s. Happy Teriyaki was our favorite lunch place near our downtown office. It was below street level, down a narrow flight of stairs. Halfway down was a cigar shop. As you descended, the sweet, earthy smell of tobacco mingled with the smell of cooking chicken, rice, and soy sauce. It kind of tickled the nose and made you feel light-headed.

The food was cheap, fast, and good. But it's the conversation that mattered. We'd sit at the undersized glass-topped tables, arguing, theorizing, gesturing with our chopsticks.

We were transforming fundraising.

Among the lunch companions at Happy Teriyaki were the authors of this book. Jeff was an account executive. Richard was our boss, co-founder of the company.

We talked about donors: What makes them give? What makes them not give? We talked about the statistics of fundraising. What truths could we pry out of the sea of numbers our work produced? We asked ourselves what shifting demographics would do to fundraising. We theorized about technology and the opportunities it would bring.

We cooked up some wild ideas. Some of them crazy-bad. A few of them revolutionary.

Those conversations were exciting and powerful. They took us places, because we were guided by two transforming principles:

1. *It's all about donors.* Fundraising works best when you work to meet donors' needs, not your own.
2. *Facts are friendly.* The more you pay attention to the facts and the data, the smarter you can be.

You'll see a lot of these two principles in this book. In fact, when I read this book, I hear echoes of those Happy Teriyaki conversations. But the principles in this book have become more practical, tempered by years of experience, strengthened by testing and refinement.

To a lot of us in fundraising, major donor work seems like a black box. Major gift officers go in and perform some kind of magic with high-end donors. (I've always had the impression that there's a lot of coffee involved.) Then money pours out. Lots of it when you do it right.

This book opens the box and reveals the mysteries of major donor fundraising. It turns out the mysteries aren't that mysterious. True, the details of major donor fundraising are different from other types of fundraising. But the core principles are the same:

▶ Put donors first.

▶ Pay attention to the facts, and don't let your personal preferences lead you astray.

▶ Work in a disciplined and methodical way—but with passion and heart.

And money pours out. A lot more of it when you pay attention to this book.

We had no inkling back when we were tossing around ideas at Happy Teriyaki that our concepts would become so real and practical. But they have, and this book is proof.

The Domain Group is gone. So is Happy Teriyaki. But the best of those cigar-and-chicken conversations live on, available to everyone who cares to pay attention.

I hope you enjoy this book as much as I have. It's engaging, realistic, and inspiring. It can help you take your major donor fundraising to new heights. And I hope you put it to work raising money for your cause—and helping your donors put their values to work.　　　　　　　　　　　　　　　　　　　　*—Jeff Brooks*

Jeff Brooks, fundraisingologist at Moceanic, has been serving the nonprofit community for nearly 30 years and blogging about it since 2005. He considers fundraising the most noble of pursuits and hopes you'll join him in that opinion.

Introduction

Five years ago, when we first published this book, we had no idea the type of positive response it would receive. What we learned is that there is a hunger in the non-profit community to understand how to do major gifts right.

And, by right we mean that major gifts, in order to be successful has to have a structure to it, parameters that help you focus correctly. Then, there must be some form of accountability for those working with major donors to help keep them disciplined and focused within that structure.

But this ONLY works when it's in the context of building authentic relationships with your major donors. You can have the best structure, discipline, accountability and even have a rock star major gift fundraiser, but unless it's all about understanding the passion and interests of the donors and matching that up with your mission…you will not be doing major gifts correctly.

We wish we could say that in the last five years every non-profit has stopped chasing the money and opted to build relationships with donors instead. This, of course is not the case. But, in the clients we serve and from the feedback we are getting from the non-profit community we ARE seeing some significant change.

But there is so much more to do! This is why we wanted to create a 2nd Edition of *It's Not JUST About the Money*.

So, what's new in this edition? Besides fixing typos and adding new graphics we've revised a number of sections dealing with the *Major Gift Pipeline* and *Qualifying Donors*. We've also created new chapters on what a *Donor Impact Portfolio* is and how it leads to dynamic offers, our new *Permission-Based Asking Model*™ and *How to Manage Up*.

So, if you read the first edition, there is plenty of new stuff in here for you. And, to top it off we think you'll actually enjoy reading our book about major gift fundraising and that it will leave you inspired!

We want to leave you though with the words we used in the introduction of our first edition because we believe they are truer today than ever.

You are the bridge between the world's greatest needs and your donors' desire and passion to address them. That is an awesome responsibility—and an equally awesome privilege. Whether you are a leader of a non-profit, the head of a development office, or a major gift officer, within these pages you will find practical, strategic information on everything from helping your donors feed their passions and realize their desires, to inspiring your team, to creating and maintaining an organization that supports a vibrant, robust major gifts program.

—Richard and Jeff

Part 1:
Discovering the Heart of Fundraising

Chapter 1:
Why People Need to Give

A wealthy industrialist once asked Mohandas Gandhi, "Do you need me or my money?" The famed Indian leader replied, "I need only you!"

Gandhi wasn't against wealth or money. But he knew that people would find neither purpose nor fulfillment in it.

Many of the great philosophers and religious leaders throughout human history have had some rather extreme, even jarring, views about money. The Bible relates that Jesus said to the rich man, "Go, sell everything you have and give to the poor, and you will have treasure in heaven." Now, that's a big ask!

But if we know anything about the heart and mind of Jesus, it's safe to assume he made that command to the rich man not only because the poor needed the man's money (though they surely did), but also because the rich man needed to give it.

Your donors, like everyone else on Earth, need to give. If we humans don't give something, somewhere, to someone, we die spiritually. That is the grace of giving. Giving is about contact with something outside of ourselves. It really isn't just about the money. And here's the great news: Your work in major gifts unlocks the grace of giving in other peoples' lives!

Most donors know instinctively that giving is good. But if you find that idea hard to swallow, here are three reasons to keep reading.

1. **Giving subdues the power of money.** Money is a powerful force. All of us feel its pull—including your donors. Money represents the hard work and the emotional investment we put into our jobs.

And it can do some great things. Money can give us options, power, security, and pleasure. It can help us express our feelings. It can allow us to provide truly important things for those we love. It can boost our self-esteem and can cause others to respect us—or so we hope.

But hold on for just a minute. Anything that is this powerful also carries a lot of potential danger. Unchecked, the influence of money can grow until it strangles a person's soul.

As a fundraiser, you help loosen money's hold on people by encouraging them to give it away. When people give away their money, they begin to short-circuit the potentially negative influence money can have in their lives. Your work of fundraising can spare people from the consequences of falling for money's sinister game. Giving also offers the donor a powerful sense of having a lasting significance, of making a difference in the world.

The people who support your organization share your values and want to participate in your work. Perhaps they wish they could do all that good work themselves, but they lack the training, talent, expertise, stamina, time, or opportunity. Or maybe they simply believe in the importance of your efforts. Either way, they want to be a partner in your work.

So, they give. They take the money they've earned through their own skills and labor and use it to fund your organization's important work. Giving allows donors to know they're doing something significant. Filtering the money, they earned doing their own work, into your organization's work makes their jobs— and their lives— more meaningful.

2. **Giving blesses the giver.** When donors give, they become deeply and immediately involved in a life beyond their own. They also confirm their deepest and truest feelings, because their behavior is guided by their hearts—the symbol of their deepest emotions and all that they care about most.

In this sense donors become linked at a spiritual level with the causes they support. The good that is accomplished as a result of a donor's charitable gifts actually becomes part of his or her life. When people give to a project, they feel connected to it. When people contribute to your organization and good things are accomplished, the hearts and lives of those donors are deeply blessed.

3. **Giving transforms lives.** Unfortunately, many nonprofit directors—and even some fundraisers—still feel reluctant to ask for money. Maybe they think asking for money is beneath them. Perhaps they just plain don't like to ask for support. These feelings are somewhat understandable. In our culture, it's not easy to talk about money. It feels embarrassing. It doesn't seem right.

But people need to give. And the more they give, the better. Why? Because giving will transform their lives—and it will transform the lives of others. And that's not just us talking. Here's what some other folks have said about giving…

"Pity may represent little more than the impersonal concern which prompts the mailing of a check, but true sympathy is the personal concern which demands the giving of one's soul." —Martin Luther King Jr.

"I have found that among its other benefits, giving liberates the soul of the giver." —Maya Angelou

"Let us not be satisfied with just giving money. Money is not enough, money can be got, but they need your hearts to love them. So, spread your love everywhere you go."
—Mother Teresa

"I hate the giving of the hand unless the whole man accompanies it." —Ralph Waldo Emerson

If you're asking honestly and using funds wisely, you have nothing to apologize for as a fundraiser. Indeed, it's your duty to ask people for their support—clearly, openly, and without apology. By doing so, you are helping to meet not only the organization's needs, but also the needs of your donors.

What's It All About?

So, fundraising really isn't just about money. But if inviting people to support your organization financially isn't all about money, what is it all about? Quite simply, it's about love. Giving is one of the deepest, most powerful, and long-lasting ways human beings can express love. It's a primary way people can live out their values and care for one another.

As a fundraiser, if you forget that, you're lost. But if you can keep that truth in your back pocket throughout your fundraising career, and if you can find ways to make that point beautifully clear to others who need to hear it, you'll find it much easier to stay encouraged and motivated.

I (Jeff) first began working in fundraising nearly thirty years ago, working for a small nonprofit that had its offices on the third floor of a dilapidated building in northwest Philadelphia. The staff was so small that I not only wrote the appeal letters but also folded them, put them in envelopes, licked the stamps, and took them to the post office. I got really good at stuffing envelopes—scary good. But the part of that job I enjoyed most was opening the returns. Because opening the mail each day allowed me to see and touch tangible expressions of our donors' gratitude.

Wait a second. Gratitude? Yes…

I remember how people would often include a short note with their gifts, expressing how overjoyed they were to help. I'll never forget looking down at the squiggly handwriting on a $5 check from an elderly woman who wrote in the memo section:

"So happy I could give this to you…" I thought about the time it must have taken her to open my letter and read what I'd written, and then to get her checkbook, write out the check and that brief note to me, and make sure the gift was sent.

At the age of twenty-three, I don't think I fully grasped the wondrously mystical connection that I experienced with our donors, people whose support went far beyond the money they gave. As I've grown more experienced and reflect back, I know that was precisely where I learned that fundraising isn't really about the money at all. It's really about an exchange of work and value.

In other words, it's about love.

Love? Seriously? Why would we get all mushy about this? Because when donors decide to give your organization even a small amount, what they are really doing is passing on to you the results of their hard work in exchange for the opportunity to make the world a better place. That's shorthand for love in our book.

Whatever great things their gifts are helping you achieve, your donors are giving you a portion of the money that also puts food on their tables, pays their bills, lets them take vacations, buys Christmas presents, sends their children to college, or helps care for their aging parents. They are handing over a part of themselves and trusting that you will use it for good.

At the moment you receive a donor's gift, something mystical is happening. Don't forget that—or overlook it. No doubt there is a lot of pressure on you simply to get the money. Pressure comes from all sides: Your boss is pushing you. Your colleagues are pressing you with their monthly goals. There's pressure from the board. It would be easy to just go after the dollars and go home.

But when you begin to feel this way, it's at those moments that you need to pause and reflect. You have a relationship with these donors. They've worked hard for what they've earned, and they happen to believe in your mission enough to give of themselves to be a part of it. You have a responsibility to love them like they love you.

Chapter 2:
Getting Your Organization Back on Track

We believe the best nonprofits are filled with people who are passionate about what they are doing. But what does that passion look like in the real world?

Well, here's what it doesn't look like: Staff members come to work lifeless. Every employee has that dull look in his or her eyes—boredom, purposelessness, fatalism. If you're part of such an organization, you may often find yourself asking, "What am I doing here?"

Good question. What are you doing? If you're an organizational leader or manager and you see this zombie-like state among your colleagues—and in yourself—there's great cause for concern.

If you're surrounded by people who seem proud that they're "in control of their emotions" or that they "never cry or express feelings," you might want to run for the door. Lack of passion in an organization, and especially in a major gifts program, can be deadly. Here are some key signs that your organization lacks passion:

- ▶ Leaders and employees are not excited about what the organization does. People are there more for the paycheck than the cause.

- ▶ There's no clear mission, purpose, or vision for the organization.
- ▶ No one talks about the people who benefit from the organization's work. Instead, they talk about themselves.
- ▶ There is a noticeable sense of ambiguity about the goals of the organization.
- ▶ Managers and leaders are more focused on process than on doing good.
- ▶ There's an absence of flexibility and creativity. Everything is in a nice, little box and very predictable. Out-of-the-box thinking is discouraged.
- ▶ The corporate culture is not supportive of employees.
- ▶ Having fun is discouraged.
- ▶ There's a lot of turf protection and lack of cooperation.

Well, that's not a pretty picture. Restrictive environments like this can suck the life out of even the most committed staff members. If this sounds a bit too much like a description of your organization, and you're in a position to make changes, here are some ideas.

Ten Steps to Getting Passion Back into Your Organization

1. Fall in love (again) with the people or cause your group serves. Who benefits from the work of your organization? What are their lives like? What do they care about? How can you do more for them?

Here's how you can encourage the staff in your organization to get the focus off of themselves and back on the people or cause you serve:

- ✔ Once a week, send an e-mail to the entire staff with a story about a dilemma faced by a person your organization serves. Usually, this will be a story that is not yet resolved.

- ✔ The purpose is to keep employees focused on why your organization exists.

- ✔ Send another e-mail each week that shares a "success story" about a person who's been helped by your organization or a situation that has improved because of your efforts. This will cement in employees' minds the significance and effectiveness of what you're doing.

- ✔ Once a month, have an employee speak to the larger group about the vision and mission of your organization and what it means to him or her. This affirms employees' investment in their work and reminds them that their efforts are important.

- ✔ Do everything possible to keep the focus on the persons helped by your organization every day. Hang photos of them in the hallways. Talk about their needs and desires in your planning meetings. Keep them always at the forefront of your employees' minds. Your entire operation is about them. If you keep that in mind, many other things will fall into place.

   2. Fall in love again with your donors. They are important stakeholders in your organization. More than the board, the executive director, or even you, it's the donors who really own the charity. Why not start behaving that way? Remind yourself and everyone you work with that, with the exception of the people who receive help from your hard work, the people who matter most are your supporters. Here are some things you can do:

- ✔ Regularly read donor letters to employees or pass along excerpts by e-mail. Focus especially on donor letters that express gratitude for being able to serve.

- ✔ Have a donor come in and speak to employees. Ask her to speak about why she got involved—and why she stays involved.

- ✔ Encourage employees to call or visit with donors so they have opportunity to hear donors' reason for supporting your organization.

3. Celebrate out-of-the-box thinking. Encourage employees to think differently, to create new opportunities or unconventional solutions to problems. Organize brainstorming sessions that allow employees to present fresh ideas and to focus broadly on new fields. Sometimes these meetings are most productive if the organizational leaders at the highest levels stay out. A freer flow of thinking gives birth to better ideas.

4. Have fun. What this looks like will vary from company to company, but having fun is always important. It may be practical jokes, random sounds broadcast on the intercom, games and competitions, going out to eat together, or just sitting around talking. Fun means laughing together and celebrating your work.

5. Publish your vision and mission. Does every employee know the organization's vision and mission? If not, it's either because these don't exist—or because you haven't publicized them. Get your vision out there. Talk about it. Explain how it came about. Remember, this is why you're together, doing what you do.

6. Create and publish your list of values. Even if you've never created a written statement of values, you have a set of values that define how the organization is run. If you don't already have a written list of values, talk about the values you share with others, create a list, and publish it. Focus on the people and causes you serve and the donors who make it all possible. And then live by those values! Ask employees to hold you and one another accountable.

7. Bring the people who are served by your organization into your work environment. There's nothing like looking into the eyes of someone whose life has been touched by the work you are doing. If possible, bring someone your group has served into the very working heart of your organization. Let him interrupt the process of the daily routine. Gather people around him to help your employees focus on what you're really doing together and why it matters. Find out what his life was like before your organization stepped in and what it's like now. What is his reaction to your involvement?

8. Keep talking—always—about both your donors and the people you serve. It needs to happen continually, not just once. It's important to keep both these groups in focus.

9. Get away from your desk and connect personally with donors and the people you serve. It's so easy to get wrapped up in the work and be stuck at your desk or in meetings all day. Plan to be absent from your desk. Put it on your calendar. Get out of your office and be with donors and the people you serve—for no reason other than to talk. Spread the joy you feel. Talk about why you're involved. Step away from your day-to-day demands and reconnect with the reason you get involved.

10. Get emotional about things. This isn't just about plans, charts, grids, logic, and the mind. It's about people. Allow your heart to be broken by the tragedies of life. Celebrate the victories. Get excited. Jump up and down. Be human. When your employees sense that you can cry and laugh, that you're real—you'll be on your way to getting passion back into the workplace.

Give yourself and your staff permission to think creatively about bringing passion back into your organization. A passionless staff means a passionless organization, and one that is on a path toward extinction.

Relationships Over Revenue

If you take only one idea from this book, make it this one—because it's at the heart of what we've discovered about how money actually works: Build relationships; don't chase bank accounts.

If your current revenue is just enough to keep your organization afloat but donor attrition is high, what does that say about the future? Fewer donors leads to less revenue, right? And that's just not sustainable.

Major gifts officers (MGOs) may find themselves wondering, "What's more important—my relationships with donors or the money they give?" We know Gandhi said people were far more important than money—and most of us would agree. But you can better understand your relationships with the people who support your organization by considering the role of money and—even more fundamentally—what money is.

One classic definition says that money is simply a medium of exchange, vested with no value other than what it is exchanged for. More than ever these days, banks across the world are discussing what backs this paper we throw around in the form of checks and bills. Is it linked to silver or gold? Should it be? But these aren't the kinds of questions worth delving into here (even if we knew the answers).

Here's what we do know. Before money existed, goods and services were exchanged directly. You might give someone two chickens and she'd give you a sack of potatoes. Or you made someone a door and some furniture, and that person would put a roof on your house. We exchanged value, not money. Now, hang on to that thought for a second.

How does a person get money these days? Mostly through labor. We earn money for the work we do. Our money represents the fruits of our own labor, the reward for our efforts. And that is the core reason why discussions about money often feel so personal and so emotional.

Money represents our labor, what we spend most of our lives doing. So, if money is a medium of exchange, and you get money through your labor, then those who give money to your organization are, in effect, working for something they believe in. People choose to fund groups that are doing what they want to see done, groups that are living up to their values and meeting their expectations in the results they produce.

This explains why donors join your cause: They want to use their labor to achieve something that matters to them. When they make a donation to your organization, they trust you'll do something they cannot do themselves. But if you don't meet those expectations, they won't see the value in transferring their hard work (through their money) to you.

So, back to the question: Is it about relationship or money? It's both. A caseload of qualified donors has a dual purpose. This graphic will show you what we mean:

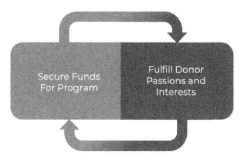

There are two operating principles that can help you bring relationships and finances together in ways that will most benefit the people you seek to serve:

The Donor-Related Principle. If your organization is properly serving a donor's needs and passions, and if there is a genuine match between those passions and the needs of the organization, the money will follow. If a person is not giving, that may mean there isn't a genuine match between the potential donor's passions and the organization's priorities. Or it may mean the donor doesn't feel properly cared for. Or financial circumstances may be preventing the donor from giving as he or she did in the past or would like to now.

If the donor's interests and your organization's goals do not match, it's time to move on. If there's a match, but the relationship is bruised because you haven't properly served the donor, it may be possible to repair it. If there's a match but there's a mitigating financial circumstance for the donor, then you need to stick with the donor—provided the next principle is met.

The Organization-Related Principle. Of course, the core objective of the major gifts officer (MGO) is to secure funds for the program. Without adequate funding, your group cannot do what you're supposed to do. Good stewardship and accountability require that an MGO focus on those relationships that will generate the most funds for the program—the relationships that will provide the best return on investment.

Most of your supporters understand this. Knowing that time is money, they don't want you investing time in them when it doesn't benefit the organization financially. And smart organizations know it, too. This is what drives the rigorous review of caseloads to see that an MGO ends up talking to the right donors—those who have the capacity to give, who want to talk, and whose passions and interests match the needs of the organization.

Putting these two principles together can help you make informed decisions where relationship and money meet. But it's not always easy! And it's not always objective. That's why you need to get to know your donors as well as you possibly can.

Make Donors Your Mission

Think again about the mission statement that's either on the wall in your office or (worse) in some dusty handbook at the bottom of your desk drawer. Yeah, that one!

Is there anything about your donors in it? Probably not. If your organization already mentions its donors in its mission statement, congratulations! That's a pretty rare occurrence. We believe that needs to change.

In fact, we believe nonprofits need to change their mission statements, so those statements not only mention donors but make donors half of their mission. There, we said it!

Sounds like crazy talk, right? But maybe radical is a better word. Such an adjustment in your mission statement represents a paradigm shift that goes way beyond being "donor-centered." It's about altering your organization's mindset and culture. In short, it's about changing the way you do business.

For too long, the nonprofit world has looked at donors as a means to an end. You need their money to get the "real work" done, right? But what if you understood your "real work" differently? What if your mission is not only about the people or cause addressed in your current mission statement but also about the need to care for, challenge, and change your donors so they can be transformed by their involvement in your work? Radical, right? Right! Such a shift will change lives and help your organization be more successful.

So, what does this new paradigm look like? Well, what if your organization actually had folks whose job was to evaluate the organization's programs and report to your donors about their impact? That's it—that's all they would do. Or what if your program people took a day each week to call or visit donors and update them on what's happening with the investment they made?

What if you invited donors to sit with your executive team in your quarterly planning meetings? Or to attend your annual retreat? What if you doubled the size of your development department so you could better reach donors who want a deeper relationship with your organization?

Do you know someone in major gifts who's working sixty hours a week and wishing there were two more people doing what they do? Or does that describe you? Just think how many donors could be reached in a more meaningful way. What if you actually had time to think, plan, and communicate with donors? What a concept!

This thinking is counter to how almost all nonprofits work, but it's time for change. The shift in organizational energy probably won't happen overnight; in most cases, it can't. But a change in the way you view donors, a change that moves beyond viewing donors as a means to an end and instead sees them as a vital part of your overall mission. That shift in mindset could happen right now. And this shift in how you understand your donors doesn't negate any of the work your organization is already doing. It allows you to keep doing it, better than ever.

The for-profit world gets this. The extraordinary companies are the ones that pay attention to people. They spend more money on their labor pool; they provide incredible customer service; and they do this without skimping on their product. Charities deliver mostly product—which is vital—but there are other things to consider.

Those extraordinary commercial companies defy conventional wisdom, yet they are wildly successful. Nonprofits can learn from this. Yes, it's a risk. Yes, it goes against the current nonprofit paradigm. But as Bob Dylan sang, "You better start swimming, or you'll sink like a stone." Are you willing to change with the times?

Chapter 3:
Building a Culture of Philanthropy

Warning: This chapter is not for the faint of heart. Building a culture of philanthropy is hard, and it often means radical change. That said, let's take a look at what a nonprofit would look, taste, and feel like if it truly embraced a healthy culture of philanthropy.

- ▶ As we discussed in the previous chapter, the mission of a healthy nonprofit organization includes its donors. Donors aren't considered a means to an end, but a vital part of the organization's work in meeting the world's greatest needs.
- ▶ All members of the organizational staff and leadership embrace the idea that fundraising is essential in fully carrying out the work and recognize that it brings joy to donors to give. Therefore, all members of the organization can ask gladly and without reservation for donors and prospective donors to give.
- ▶ Board members are the nonprofit's biggest cheerleaders and unceasingly ask those within their "sphere of influence" to join them in the cause that is so dear to their hearts.

- ▶ It's hard to tell who's working in "program" and who is in "development." Staff in each area have respect for the other's work, and willingly and enthusiastically help understand each other's needs.
- ▶ Donors trust the organization. They feel cared for, loved, challenged, thanked, educated, valued, and involved in part of the solution. They don't feel talked down to, but rather are constantly reminded of how important their involvement is to address the need.
- ▶ Everyone in the organization knows "the story." The story is about why the organization exists, both the pain and the joy. "The story" is engrained in the hearts and minds of all who are connected to the organization and is told over and over, again and again—and it makes them beam with pride and choke with tears.
- ▶ Walking through the doors of this nonprofit, a person feels love, empathy, righteous anger, grace, hard work, personal care, and ... more love.

Who wouldn't want to be part of an organization like that? But about now, you're thinking, "This is just a dream. It could never be like this in my organization."

Guess what? You're wrong. If this is what you want, you can create it. Do this, and your staff will be happier, donors will be more connected, and your programs will be easier to fund.

The Donor as Part of Your Mission

Today, in the keynote speech at any fundraising conference or in every article about fundraising you read, you'll find people talking about being "donor-focused" or "donor-centered." Everyone talks about how important this is, but in most cases, it doesn't really change the way we operate.

Nonprofit leaders talk a good game. They try to thank donors promptly, figure out what their supporters are interested in, and send out quarterly newsletters to show people how their gifts have made a difference.

But to be blunt, donors are still being treated as a means to an end. To create a true culture of philanthropy in our organizations, donors have to be part of the mission—not a way to get our mission accomplished, but an actual part of the mission. That means:

- ▶ Donors are actually included in the organization's mission statement. Yes, among the reasons your organization exists is to help transform your donors and to allow them to help transform the world.

- ▶ The organization understands that its role is really to become a bridge between the world's greatest needs and donors' passion to meet those needs. The donor and the need cross over that bridge to meet each other. Your role is to knock down any barriers that could get in the way.

- ▶ The organization isn't interested in the ratio between "program" and "development," but rather in results and impact. You know donors are interested in making a difference in the world. They want to invest in programs that actually work. To have programs that work, you hire quality people and provide them with the tools they need.

- ▶ Half of the organization's time, energy, and resources is devoted to donors. You believe donors are part of your mission, and your organization is devoted to helping transform donors by allowing them to know and feel the impact of their philanthropy.

- ▶ In all conversations with staff about programs, projects and need, these two questions are always asked: "Will our donors think this is a good idea?" and "Will our donors feel this is a good investment?"

- ▶ Donors have a seat at the table. You value their input, opinions, and ideas on how to make your organization more effective. You provide opportunities for your staff to hear their voices.

- ▶ The organization is not afraid to ask for financial support. You realize donors want to help you change the world, and you are bold in asking for their help.
- ▶ Everyone in the organization has a relationship with donors. You realize donors are not just cared for by "development professionals." Instead, the entire staff is called into relationship with donors. Staff members have respect for one another's roles, yet all of you understand that everyone has a responsibility to donors, because they are part of your mission.
- ▶ Donors are celebrated. And that doesn't just mean at an annual banquet or a ribbon cutting, but in small, everyday ways—in meetings, with the little note from a program person, or a picture sent from a major gifts officer. And this isn't a "strategy"; it's just the way you do it.

What is Leadership's Role?

Let's be absolutely clear. If donors are part of your mission—which, as we've said, is essential if you really want a culture of philanthropy in your organization—then the leadership of your organization must have a passionate desire to be in relationship with donors and to ask donors for their involvement.

If leaders refuse to be in relationship with donors, or simply cannot bring themselves to relate to donors (for whatever reason), they should be fired. Yes, fired.

Think about it in the for-profit world. Would the CEO of a company last if he or she didn't care about customers or shareholders? Are you kidding? No way! Yet, in the nonprofit world we put up with it. Right now, in nonprofits all over this country, staff members are sitting around tables trying to figure out how to work around the fact that leadership is not on board with where the fundraising team is headed. It's so dysfunctional.

You'll hear board members justify it by saying, "Well, our executive director is terrible at fundraising, but he's so good at developing programs and being innovative in the field."

So, what! If leaders can't inspire people to fund their innovations, they'll never get off the ground.

It all goes back to understanding who donors are in relationship to your organization. If donors are part of your mission and leadership embraces this concept, then leadership is actively and passionately establishing relationships with donors. They recognize that the good work they are seeking to accomplish cannot happen without donors. They also know that donors need your organization to fulfill their own need of wanting to change the world.

Unless leadership understands this—and acts out of that understanding—the organization will be out of balance and will fall into dysfunction.

Note that this is also about the governing board—not just the president or executive director. If you're on the board of directors of a nonprofit, you have to give of your resources. Be it $10 or $10 million, you have to give. You also have to embrace the concept, along with the nonprofit's leadership team, that donors are crucial to the mission of the organization. And this means that you, as a board member, have to be an ambassador for that nonprofit.

This means inviting those in your "sphere of influence" into a relationship with your organization. If you're not willing to do this, you shouldn't be on a board—no matter how great you are in accounting, law, or program. If you can't give and invite others to participate, then you don't really believe the organization is worthy of support.

Organizations with a true culture of philanthropy have staff leaders and board members who are passionate about donors. This ensures that no matter who goes in or out of the organization, this passion will never die. The board will never allow a president to come in without that passion, and a president will never recruit a board member who doesn't have it.

This is critical, people. Are you listening? Without your inspiration and passion for donors and the need, you make it so much harder for your team to be successful.

Telling Your Story

Do you know your organization's story? Do you know how it began and why it exists? Have you ever considered why people support your organization? You'd be surprised at how many nonprofit staff members don't.

But if your organization desires a true culture of philanthropy, everyone involved must know your story. It's your story that brings you together as a team around a common mission. Your story explains why you exist. Telling that story on a regular basis is critical for your staff, board, and donors. It keeps you focused on who you are and prevents you from straying off course.

So, what is telling your story all about? Quite simply, it's an account of the collective acts that bring together all constituents— staff, board, donors, volunteers, and community—around a shared mission. You tell your story in many different ways: in written form in all of your communications, in presentations to donors, and in the way your organization treats its staff and those you serve. The story is about who you are and what you're doing to make the world a better place.

Here are six practical ways to tell your story.

- ✔ Spend quality time getting your story right. Make sure it's written well, that leaders can tell it with passion and conviction, and that it stirs the heart.

- ✔ Place your mission, vision, and values prominently in the foyer of your office space. That way anyone walking in knows what you're about.

- ✔ Create an "Our Story" piece that goes into your employee handbook, your board orientation folder, and on your website.

- ✔ Start every staff and board meeting with a segment that

retells or emphasizes some portion of your story as an organization. This reiterates over and over again your mission, vision, and values. It reminds the people involved of why your organization exists.

✔ Create engagement events and touch points that allow donors and volunteers to hear your story, to talk about it together, and to get involved in writing the next chapter.

✔ Tell your story over and over, to everyone who will engage with you, lest anyone forget. Tell it in meetings, in the elevator, at galas, on face-to-face donor visits, to your significant others. This is important.

It Takes a Village

In order to build a positive philanthropic culture, you need to have everyone "on the bus" with you. It's not just about leaders; everyone needs to be moving in the same direction. This should include:

- Development staff;
- Board and committee members;
- Program staff;
- Support staff; and
- Donors

We have repeatedly heard fundraisers lament that "Our program staff want nothing to do with fundraising. They think all we care about is money. They're constantly complaining about how we talk about 'their' work."

But when we talk to program folks, their refrain is, "Those people in development have no clue what we do. They never come around unless they want to show us off to a donor. It really bugs us."

Sound familiar? If your organization has a true culture of philanthropy, everyone sits together at the development table. Every person in the organization has a clear understanding of the importance donors play in the mission. Similarly, staff members who work primarily in development understand program—they feel it, taste it, and live it to appreciate it on a regular basis. As a fundraiser, you have to know what you're asking donors to support.

And let's not forget about support staff. Many times, these folks are forgotten, but support staff are incredibly important in that they are often the first contact people have with your organization. Do your front desk people know how to speak with a donor who walks through the door? Do members of your support staff really understand why they are being asked to help hand-address envelopes to donors? That may sound trivial, but it's not.

Too often, support staff get irritated when they're asked to help with certain tasks that involve donors. When that happens, it usually indicates that the organization has actually done these people a disservice by not communicating the importance of fundraising and the role of the donor. The attitude you want from all staff is one of service, both to donors and to the people you serve. Here are some concrete ideas for building a culture of philanthropy among all your staff:

- ✔ When you hire a new staff person, have an extensive discussion about the role donors and philanthropy play in your organization. Actually, it's best if that conversation happens in the interview process. You don't want to hire someone who's uncomfortable with donors.

- ✔ Codify, in your employee handbook, how you work with donors and what the role of fundraising is in your organization. Include information about the importance of thanking donors properly; the role of staff at development events; the relationship between program and development, and the critical role the board plays in building a healthy organization.

- ✔ Invite donors to some of your staff meetings to hear a new perspective.

- ✔ Invite donors to a planning meeting. They'll have a lot to add.
- ✔ Take program staff on donor visits and solicitations. Use the expertise of your program folks to "sell" the donors on a project.
- ✔ At staff meetings, tell donor stories. Organizations often do a great job telling stories about programs but often overlook the stories of donors. Tell them.
- ✔ Invite donors to your organization's celebrations. The more opportunities you provide for staff, board, and donors to come together, the more appreciation there will be for one another.

These are some concrete ways to create a thriving culture of philanthropy within your organization with your staff. It can be difficult, but you honestly have no choice. If you don't create this type of atmosphere, your organization won't be around in ten years.

Pause for Thought:
Everyone Needs an Excuse
Jeff Schreifels

Over the many years we have been working with clients we have found it's quite beneficial for the development staff to get out of the office and do a retreat with colleagues. So, while you're thinking about it, start planning a time away from the office with your coworkers and do something different. You don't have to call it a retreat if you don't want to but spending a couple of days away from your normal existence at work has some tremendous benefits. Here's a list of some of the benefits you will experience:

You get to wear casual clothing. You might not think this is a big deal, but I'm talking about wearing shorts and sandals. Psychologically, it allowed us to relax a bit and feel more informal.

It sounds weird, but people behaved differently. It's almost like the real person comes out when they're not in the office "uniform."

You became more human with one another. While discussing a number of really important topics, you will begin to tell each other your own stories. It will be powerful, and it will carry on throughout the day, into lunch and dinner. People will really open up, and you'll encounter a lot of emotions, even tears. Far from feeling uncomfortable, it will create a sense of empathy and shared concern. We don't always get to do that in an office setting.

You really listen to one another. I think we don't often create spaces in our work environments to sit down and actually listen to one another, busy as we are with the task at hand.

Sometimes our agenda is so important, we don't actually want to hear what our colleagues have to say. We need time and freedom to listen, to talk, and to listen some more. It will build up amazing trust.

Your team will become more unified. There will be a couple of moments when you'll really sense the team coming together around some issues that, in the past, had previously been hard to even talk about. You'll see colleagues supporting each another. Speaking freely about their failures. I never hear that in the office. Folks will be able to be vulnerable, which empowers others to do the same.

You'll genuinely get to know one another better. Because you shared a number of meals together and had some informal time to talk about who you were, it will enable each of you to know your colleagues just a little more. This is what each of us wants, including our donors—we want to be known.

You tell donor stories. For us, this was probably the best part. Throughout the course of the day, you will be able to share your favorite story about something a donor said or did. Some were hilarious, others will bring tears to your eyes. At the end of the day, you will once again be renewed with the sense that each of us truly understood what your work was all about. It will be a really powerful time.

It doesn't have to cost a lot of money to do something like this. It could be as simple as going to the home of one of your colleagues, or even to a donor's workplace conference room. The point is to spend some time away from your normal environment and experience something different with the people you work with. It's incredibly productive, and you'll leave inspired to tackle the hard work you have waiting for you back at the office.

Chapter 4:
Taking Your Donor to the Need

In our work with development professionals, we will often speak with MGOs who feel stuck in their relationship with a certain donor. No matter what the staff member does, he just can't seem to get that donor engaged. He even knows what she's most interested in, but nothing seems to work. Our conversation with the MGO normally goes something like this: Us: *Did you take her there?* MGO: *Where?*

Us: *Did you take her to the scene?* MGO: *What scene?*

Us: *Did you take her into the need? Did you invite her into the lives of the people you're trying to help?*

MGO: *No, she won't go. She's not interested in visiting any of our program locations.*

Us: *But you can still take her. You can take her with your words, and pictures, and videos. You can transport her right into the scene!*

Sounds good. But the idea of using words and images to replicate the experience of actually being there is easier said than done. It's difficult to help donors cross the line from their comfort zones right into the hurt and pain of the need you are addressing. But if you do it right, if you allow donors to experience the need with all their senses, you will grab their hearts in a most dramatic way.

I (Richard) remember being part of a groundbreaking ceremony for The Salvation Army's Door of Hope program in San Diego. This program helps homeless mothers and their children get their lives back together. I expected a straightforward ceremony with speeches, music, and presentations—plus the obligatory shovel of dirt. I was sitting in the back, enjoying a sunny San Diego afternoon as I listened to the program. Then a mom got up and told her story. It was a dramatic story of pain, abuse, injustice, loneliness, and hurt. My stomach was in a knot. And then there was redemption and restoration as I heard how the Salvation Army helped to bring the warm, bright light of love and care into this awful and seemingly hopeless situation. I looked around at the other moms and kids, some peering out of the doorways and windows of the buildings behind us. And I broke down and cried. It grabbed me. The need just grabbed me.

While hearing a story doesn't have the same impact as actually being there, if you can faithfully replicate what you see and feel when you're in a program location, you'll be more likely to get your donor's attention and, more importantly, his heart—which is the driving factor in the whole decision-making process.

But talking about the need isn't always easy. Here's why:

- ▶ You may not know all the facts. You need to be curious about the need. You need to want to know more. If you don't, you should ask yourself why.

- ▶ It's emotionally difficult to be close to the need. To overcome this, you might have to examine your own issues, reactions, and feelings, and how they affect your ability to get close to the need.

- ▶ You are concerned about exploiting the very people you seek to serve. The "PC police" are in your head and in your office, telling you that using vivid language and provocative images to relay the need amounts to "poverty porn." As a result, you and your organization may think it's better to focus more on opportunity (smiling faces) than on the real struggles the people you serve are facing. But the truth is that presenting opportunity (smiling faces) doesn't communicate as powerfully as showing real need. It just doesn't. We are wired, as humans, to respond to need. It's logical, and it's right. Transporting the donor into the suffering while protecting the dignity of the people in question is a matter of speaking to the people involved and asking their permission to tell their stories.

▶ You really don't think it's possible to make a difference. If you really believe this, maybe it's time to find another job. Or it could be that you've forgotten that real change can happen when people come together for a common good. The Irish philosopher and statesman Edmund Burke once said, "The only thing necessary for the triumph of evil is for good people to do nothing." He also stated, "Nobody made a greater mistake than he who did nothing because he could only do a little." The fact is that every little bit helps. And little by little, we will change the world—when all of us do our part.

Zeroing in on the Need

Take a moment to think about what it feels like when you visit a program site. At first, there may be some talk about what's happening: "Here's what we're doing…" But then, if you really allow yourself to focus on the actual need, things begin to change.

There are a variety of emotions. Anger. Sadness. Empathy. It may make you uncomfortable. If your cause involves direct service to people in need, you may find it very hard to look into the eyes of those folks. You might try to disguise your reactions to what you're seeing or feeling. You may worry about whether you are saying or doing the right things. What is the other person thinking?

All these responses are natural reactions to the hurt and pain we see in others. It is at once pulling us in to help and pushing us away to escape.

I (Richard) remember a conversation I once had with a man at a homeless shelter. He was dirty and smelled bad. He had a certain shiftiness about him, a street-smart persona that I didn't quite trust. At first, I didn't want to be close to him. He made me very uncomfortable. I kept thinking about all that I had and all that he didn't. Guilt—that was it. Why were things so good for me and so bad for him?

Then we sat and talked. I realized he wasn't sure what to think of me, either. He looked at me and thought, "What does this man want? What's he going to do? Is he just going to use me? Can I trust him?"

As we talked more, I could see him begin to relax. So, did I. I didn't notice the dirt as much. Or the smell. Now we were just two fathers sitting together talking about the journey.

It's important to train yourself to focus on the need when visiting program sites—because that focus helps drive everything you do in fundraising. It drives:

▶ A clear understanding of what the problem is in human and emotional terms. The whole point of a nonprofit is to solve problems—all kinds of problems. When you focus on the need, you gain a very clear view of what you are trying to do.

▶ The ability to remember what the main point is. It's amazing to me how quickly we forget the primary point of our work. We fall victim to the tendency to define our job as "raising money" or "managing fundraising and marketing" instead of what it truly is—to help solve a problem or address a need.

▶ A proper balance of head and heart. A fix on the need keeps your heart engaged, and that is very important. You can have all of the logic, planning, to-do lists, and numbers just right, but if your heart is cold, you won't be a successful fundraiser. And the way you keep your heart warm is to be in contact with the need all the time. It keeps you balanced, focused, and properly aligned.

So, once you're sure your heart is engaged and you have the right focus on the need, the next step is to relate that need to your donors. Try this little exercise.

Sit down and begin to write about the need. Don't start with solutions. Instead, simply write down the answer to the question, "What is the need we're seeking to address?" Try it. Just describe the need. But be warned: It's not easy.

Now, go back and read over what you've just written. Did you describe it in emotional and human terms? Or did you use a lot of head language like, "This situation is part of a social trend in this area…" Such language has its place, but many organizations use it far too frequently. Instead, focus on what it feels like to be in this situation. What do people experience because of this problem? What are you experiencing because you're in this situation?

Don't worry about political correctness. This isn't the time to be asking yourself, "Should I be saying that?" Describing the need is more difficult than you think. That's because it is so painful and disturbing—as it should be. Let yourself go into the need, the pain, the hurt. It will be good for you personally and professionally.

Identifying and Talking About the Cause of the Need

Now it's time to step back a little bit, to shift the focus from the heart to the head and identify the cause of the need.

Often, in this journey of helping others or our planet, we can wax eloquent about the need and about what we're doing, while remaining truly ignorant about the real causes of the problem we are seeking to address.

For a fundraiser, this lack of understanding may not become a real problem until someone (often a donor or potential donor) asks us the question, "Well, why do you think this happens?" Or maybe the question is a bit less direct: "You know, my husband and I were talking about this the other night. Now, don't get me wrong, we really want to help, but we were wondering …" If you're not ready to respond with an answer, you'll find yourself in an uncomfortable place. And if you've not given it some careful thought beforehand, you'll be tempted to wing it, which is never a good idea.

For some of us, it's easy to get all fired up about addressing need. But when it comes to the kind of complex problems many charities seek to address, we also need to spend time making sure we have an intellectual grasp of the causes of that need. Being familiar with causes of the need will increase your confidence in talking with donors about your work.

The old adage, "Information tells, emotion sells," applies here. In thinking through these causes, you are trying to gather information that the donor will need to set the context for really understanding the importance of your group's work. Then you'll be ready to move to draw the connection between what she wants to do with her resources and what your organization is doing.

To make sure you have a handle on the causes of the need, take some time to go through the following steps:

- ▶ Write down the need at the top of a piece of paper.
- ▶ Make a list of some of the causes or contributing factors that come to mind. For instance, if the need is hunger, your list may include civil unrest, bad government, poor natural resources, lack of money, injustice, greed, etc. Google the cause. You can come up with more ideas on causes by researching the topic. Add those to your list.
- ▶ Sit with your list. Is it right? Have you included everything? You might consult some other people and ask their opinions. Ask a program person what he or she thinks. Remember, the goal is to get a comprehensive list.
- ▶ Avoid technical jargon. "Jargonizing" the need is a way of escaping it. Your explanation of the causes of the need should be simple enough for a fifth-grader to understand. If it isn't, keep working at it.
- ▶ Choose the top five causes. This will help you focus your

attention on the major reasons so you can be ready to talk about them. Share your top five with others familiar with the situation and see if they ring true. Go back to the program person and to your colleagues and share your conclusions. Do they agree? If so, you're ready to move on.

Documenting What Will Happen if the Need is Not Met

When you were a child, you probably heard your mom say something like, "If you don't eat your vegetables, you can't have any cake." You either learned to believe it when she said it or, if it was just a veiled threat, you learned to ignore it.

This dynamic is true in most of life. We pay attention to avoiding real consequences. And we quickly learn what threats are not real.

Perhaps your boss says, "George, we cannot have you coming in late every morning. If this pattern continues, I'll be forced to let you go." But you keep coming in late, and nothing happens. And you quickly learn that the boss didn't really mean it. Or, if he did, he didn't have the courage to follow through.

These experiences, which happen to us in every area of life, train us to be a bit skeptical about what people say will happen if we don't act. Sometimes people make promises (or threats) and then they don't follow through. Before long, no one tends to believe that what those people are saying will happen.

Donors are becoming more skeptical, too. Gone is the day when a major donor simply believes what she's told by the organization she's supporting.

Here's how this relates to the dynamic of taking the donor to the scene. So far, you've carefully described the need in emotional, human terms. You've intelligently articulated the causes of the need. Now you have to take the next step and speak about what will happen if the need isn't met. This can be difficult for various reasons:

▶ You may not know with any certainty what will happen if the need isn't met.

- You may not really believe anything negative will happen if you do not address the need. Maybe you believe some other organization or person will step in and meet the need, if your group does not. (Be honest. This is a touchy one because if you really do believe this, then why are you working there?)
- You can't bring yourself to really think about what will happen if the need is not met.
- It's uncomfortable to talk about such things. We may know that unless we act, children will die of starvation, or political prisoners will be tortured, or more people will remain homeless. But it's not pleasant to talk about such things. The PC police, either in reality or in your head, have shown up on the scene to properly direct things and make sure everything stays neat and tidy.

Any of these can be a very understandable reason to get stuck here. But it's important to take proactive steps to move beyond this point and get comfortable with talking about what will happen if the need is not met. Here are some suggestions on what you can do:

- Engage in a conversation on this topic. Include program people, the leaders in the organization, front-line managers who are delivering your solutions, and your fundraising colleagues. It will be good for all of you to get a grasp on the consequences of failing to meet the need.
- Confront the voice in your head that says, "Nothing will really happen if we don't meet this need." If you are feeling this way, share those feelings with others whom you trust, because this will help you process it. But be careful not to silence the question completely. It's always good to ask whether the programs we're asking donors to support actually make a difference. If you refuse to consider that question, then you'll have a hard time convincing donors that your work is worth their support. Strive to tame that

little voice but not silence it.

Embrace the fact that you are a critical part of the organization's solution. You're helping to secure the resources and the good will of donors who want to help. And since you and your colleagues and your donors have agreed to do something about this need, you share responsibility for the outcome. This is serious business. So, it's helpful to spend constructive time considering what will happen if the need is not met.

Becoming Part of the Solution

So, you've learned how to take your donor into the need. By now, she is keenly aware of what the need is, why the need exists, and the consequences of the need not being met. So, she has a firm grasp of the situation. More importantly, she feels the need and is totally engaged. She has an urgency about her, an energy you may not have seen before. And she wants to take action. Her desire to "do something" is an important sign that you've done this part of your job well.

Once your potential donor is emotionally and intellectually engaged, once you sense that she sees and, even more importantly, feels the need, it's time to talk about how she can be a part of addressing that need. Here's what you need to do:

✔ ***Tell the donor what your organization plans to do to meet this need.*** This is where you describe the program plan—the solution to the need. It needs to be specific with deadlines and outcomes. You need to explain your plan in simple (but not simplistic) and practical terms. Avoid any jargon and just speak plainly with the donor about what you're going to do, when you're going to do it, and what you expect the outcomes to be. Don't make the outcomes a general statement ("we will address the problem of homelessness"). Be specific about what will happen ("15 formerly homeless women will be given transitional housing and trained for employment"). Lack of specifics at this point can be a real deal-breaker. There is nothing more frustrating to a potential donor than when a staff person starts to babble in generalities when it comes to what their work will accomplish. When you do that, you're telling the donor that either (a) you really don't know what you're doing, or (b) you don't have a conviction about responding to the need.

- ✔ *Tell the donor what it will cost.* This is the budget. Again, specifics are good here. An easy-to-understand budget with practical categories that are easy to understand is critical. Your finance department may use particular language for its purposes; that doesn't mean you can't use different language to describe those same budget lines in your proposal. Use words that will communicate to your potential donor.

- ✔ *Invite the donor to get involved.* This is "the ask." This is the key moment when you go back and remind the donor about the need and assure her of the difference her gift will make in addressing it. This is also the time when you remind her of the consequences of your failing to meet that need.

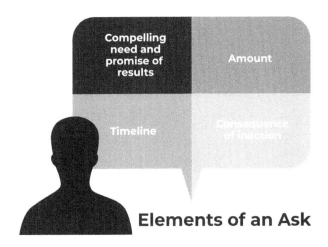

Elements of an Ask

There are four essential elements to an effective ask:

1. A compelling description of the need and what the gift will accomplish (the promise);
2. A specific amount;
3. A timeline for when the gift is needed; and
4. A description of what will happen if help is not received.

It's very important to make sure these four elements are part of every ask you make.

A Final Secret

Transporting your donor to the scene is really a two-part process. The first part is focused on properly describing and documenting the need for the work you are doing. The second part is all the other stuff. But here is something that we've learned: If you get the need part right, you can make a lot of mistakes on the second part and still come out alright. If you are able to present a powerful case regarding the need, your donor will be so compelled that he or she will give you "room" if other parts of your appeal are less effective.

Don't misunderstand—you should make every effort to be sure the rest of it is right. But in relative terms, you need to get the "need part" really right. Spend the majority of your time on that.

Pause for Thought:
The Power of Yes—and No
Richard Perry

Yes and No. We have two thoughts about these very important words. The first thought is focused on who you are. The second involves how you behave. Let's start with the "who."

We have met and worked with so many different types of personalities in our business. To be honest, it's invigorating and frustrating at the same time.

But over the years, we've encountered two distinct types of people whose personalities have made an impression on us and have also served as predictors of their success in fundraising.

Yes People vs. No People

When it comes to dealing with problems, mistakes, obstacles, and challenges, Yes People look at the situation and respond with an attitude that says, "Yes, let's figure out how to overcome this and create a solution." No People, on the other hand, say, "No, this is a big problem and I can't see any way to make it work."

Which kind of person are you? Do you ever notice that when you're at a party or even just having lunch with a group of co-workers, there are certain people whom others just seem to gravitate towards? Those are the Yes People. They exude positivity and are pleasant to be around. Their outlook on work and life is genuine—and that is key. Yes People are the real deal. They're confident but humble. They have great energy yet are aware of their surroundings and the feelings of other people. They tackle problems with a great attitude yet understand their enormity.

When we interview prospective MGOs and other development professionals, this yes attitude is the first thing we look for. We know from experience that Yes People are successful. Of course, experience and knowledge are important. But we've seen people who have no background in working with major donors or fundraising succeed immediately because they have such a tremendous attitude and outlook. What these people don't have in experience or knowledge, they'll soon figure out how to get. We've seen this happen many, many times.

So, what if you take a long and honest look at yourself and realize that you are more of a No Person, even though you might desire to be a Yes Person? Here are some thoughts. But be warned, it's hard stuff:

Perhaps you're in the wrong profession. We have found that many individuals who seem like *No People* turn into *Yes People* the minute they find what truly brings them joy.

Consider seeing a professional counselor. Counseling gives you honest feedback from a skilled professional that allows you to "go deep." It can be incredibly painful, but if you can work with the process, it can also be incredibly rewarding.

Ask a friend you trust to speak truth into your life. If you have someone in your life who is willing to be honest with you, someone who will tell you if he or she senses something is wrong, ask that individual what kind of person he or she believes you to be. It can be scary but hearing the truth about who you are can change you.

Personally examine your own life. This may mean taking 15 to 30 minutes a day to sit in quiet, or it may involve taking a block of time away for an extended retreat. What is most important is that you take the time to examine who you are, why you do what you do, and where you're going. Most of us are so busy "doing," we never take the time to just "be." This kind of self-examination might sound religious, but that's not necessarily true.

On the other hand, it is definitely spiritual. All of us have a spiritual side to ourselves in addition to our mental and emotional sides. In order to be successful at our jobs and in life in general, we need to take care of all these facets of who we are.

It's nearly impossible for No People to be successful in major gifts fundraising. Colleagues don't want to seek or follow their advice, and donors ultimately don't respond to them. Yes People see what is possible, embrace hardships, and work to overcome them. And hardships, as you know, can occur on a regular basis in this profession. The good news is, even if you see yourself as a No Person at this time, you can turn it around. You can become a Yes Person.

Turning Their "No" into Your "Yes"

Regardless of whether you're a *No* Person or a *Yes* Person, you are occasionally going to encounter setbacks. No fundraiser has a 100 percent success rate on her fund appeals. As a fundraiser, sometimes you will make your best effort, offer a powerful and well planned ask, and the response will be a "no."

Most of us have been taught that a "no" indicates failure. And none of us like to fail. At some level, we all fear failure, as well as the hurt and shame that often come with it.

But failure can actually be a building block of success; we just have to re-orient our way of thinking about it. Great achievements are almost always preceded by failures. And note that we said failures—with an "s" on it. Many failures.

Did you know that in the business world, the ratio between ideas and successful product introductions is 1,200 to 1? You might look at that ratio and conclude that there wasn't much of value in those other 1,199 ideas. You might see them simply as a long list of failures. Or you could see that the truth is that each time you try something and don't fully succeed, you're learning more and more about (a) what doesn't work, and (b) what might work next time. Success is always preceded by failure.

In other words, a "no" is nothing more than a step on the journey to a yes. No closes a door, which enables us to turn our attention to the next door. You know, the door that's standing open right beside the door you were knocking on—the open door you can't see because you're so focused on the door that's closing? Yeah, that door.

The failures and no's we encounter in our lives can be either huge monsters or wonderful gifts. It depends on how we choose to look at them.

So, as you're looking at your work in major gifts fundraising, think about this. Are the no's stealing your spirit and drive? Is your fear of failure immobilizing you?

Why not begin to see these "no" moments as the good friends they are? A "no" from a donor can mean so many things:

- No, not now.
- No, not that.
- No, wrong amount.
- No, I have a concern.
- No, I have other priorities.

Each of these answers provides you with information you can use. What a wonderful thing to find out which "no" it is! No matter what the explanation, there's a positive benefit to each no. Either you have an opportunity to adjust the timing, project, or amount, or you find out there's a problem that needs to be addressed, or you find out that this donor is no longer interested. Whatever the case, you've got a productive next step you can take. Now you know what to do!

So, go out there and find as many no's as you can. They are your friends—really!

Chapter 5:
Pitfalls to Avoid

As you seek to create an organizational culture that places donors at the center of your mission, you may be tempted to look to other groups to help you figure out what an effective major gift program looks like.

Not a bad idea. "Steal smart" is a time-honored business precept. But just because another organization is doing things differently, it doesn't necessarily mean it's doing them better. Or right.

Here is a variety of ways organizations get it wrong—and some suggestions for how you can avoid falling into the same traps.

Pitfall 1:

Putting program over people. Have you ever sat in a staff meeting with the program, finance, or fundraising folks, and realized that no one is talking about the people the organization exists to serve, or the problem it's seeking to address? You spend two hours in a conference room discussing your work, but no one mentions the woman who's been abused, the man addicted to drugs, the hungry child, the cancer patient, the person with disabilities, the endangered species, the environmental disaster, etc.

Instead, it's all about the latest processes, criteria, charts, trends, and studies.

It's all good stuff, in the proper place. But what's often missing is heart, emotion, empathy, and concern—the things that make us human and remind us what it's all about.

In our consulting work with nonprofits, we sometimes meet with groups who speak of their work only in terms of process, logistics, and criteria. It's no surprise that, when we read the proposals and offers that their major gifts officers have been cranking out, they feel devoid of any humanity or emotional language. Their fundraising acts on the stage that had already been set—with a focus on process, criteria, facts, and numbers. Not surprisingly, these major gifts officers were unsuccessful in raising money.

As we've studied this dynamic, we've realized that every non-profit begins with a mission but, over time, they often migrate to a fixation on process. The result is that people and heart take a back seat on a journey that leads nowhere.

Don't misunderstand. Process, charts, and numbers are all absolutely essential to running a successful program. But they've never raised a dime.

When process dominates our internal communications, it invariably begins to show in how we talk to our donors. If you talk about the logistics of running the program and not the reason why the program exists and is important, don't be surprised if donors lose motivation and response dips.

If your job tasks are focused primarily on administration or finances, it can be easy to lose sight of the real reason you do the work you do. That's why we encourage all staff in nonprofits to stop each week and spend at least a little time thinking about the people your organization serves: the homeless person, the hungry child, the person fighting cancer, the forgotten elderly, the communities facing environmental destruction. Be gripped by the dangers they face, the hurt and pain they feel. Allow your heart to break. Cry with them. And then, through your efforts, experience the joy of helping. Don't ever forget them.

This isn't complicated—it may even seem obvious—but it's incredibly important. If you lose sight of the people or cause your organization seeks to serve, you run the risk of thinking that your creativity, your strategy, and your brilliance are what the mission is all about. You become fixated on the process of doing rather than the people and causes you're seeking to serve. It's too easy to migrate into process and the program, and end up creating good marketing materials that lack any real heart. It's essential that you be aware of this dynamic so you can avoid letting it creep into your head and your work. Keep the heart and humanity in your thoughts, your language, your writing, and your donor communications. If you lose the heart for your cause, you've lost everything.

When we are in touch with our own pain and loneliness, we can properly love those around us and be present with those we serve. Even in those times when you do need to focus on process, stop occasionally just to remember the people. Here are four very simple, very specific things you can do to foster the "people focus" in your organization.

- ✔ Every morning before you start your day, think about the people or cause your nonprofit serves. Be thankful for them and vow that today, you'll keep in mind their joys and pains, their hopes and needs, and you'll find a way, through your fundraising efforts, to do your part to help them.

- ✔ Make sure the people or causes you serve are present in every meeting you're in. Tell a story about a problem you encountered or a solution that worked. Or, simply say, "Let's go back to square one for a little while and think about the impact on the people or cause we serve."

- ✔ Make sure the people you serve are represented in every donor communication, whether verbal or written. Make sure the people or cause is the first thing on your lips or in the headline of the document.

✔ At least once a week find a story about the struggle or victory that a person or the cause you serve has encountered. Let it break your heart, renew your sense of purpose, and fill you with sheer joy of knowing you have the privilege to help.

If you do these four things, you will avoid sliding into complacency, hardness of heart, and mediocrity. Instead, you'll stay grounded and centered where you should be—with a soft and caring heart for the people and causes you're committed to serving. There is no better place to be, and it will help you be more successful in your job.

Pitfall 2:

Putting money over relationships. At one point or another, nearly everyone has had some sort of pretty serious struggle with money—wanting it, needing it, being controlled by it, or letting it blur our values and judgment. We fear we won't have enough money to be secure, so we obsess about it. There's no doubt money drives things in our personal as well as professional lives. And in the nonprofit world, it's a delicate balance. Here are three ways nonprofits can go terribly wrong in relation to money:

1. *We view donors as sources of cash rather than as partners.* We don't intend to do so, but we sometimes fall into the trap of reducing our donors to I.D. numbers on a list instead of real human beings. Sometimes our agenda is just to take the money and run. We all know it's ultimately a deadend street, but often we end up behaving this way because we feel so much pressure to meet financial goals.
2. *We function as if revenue is more important than helping others.* So, we spend more time focused on finances—talking about them, worrying about them, emphasizing them—than on the people or causes we've committed ourselves to.
3. *We view money as the objective, when it should be an outcome.* If earning money is the only reason you work,

there's trouble ahead. If a business owner's single objective is to earn money, disaster is looming around the corner. If all you care about in your relationship to your donors is their ability to fund your program, your job is headed for failure.

In healthy settings, money is an outcome of doing the right thing. It's a by-product of effectively serving your employer, customer, or donor. Yet it's so easy just to chase the money! Any non-profit will hit the skids if its leaders shift their focus away from the cause and give primary attention to chasing funding sources. It may take some years, but eventually things will start to go bad.

If it's happening to you or your organization, don't despair. It's only natural. Just take the reins now. Here's what you can do now to counter this very normal and natural tendency in the major gifts and fundraising field.

- ✔ Get in touch with your own fears and security issues. Do you fear you might fail or lose your job? Are you afraid of not having enough cash? Do you ache when people perform better or earn more than you do? We all have these anxieties, so they are nothing to be ashamed of. But if they're controlling your life, admit it to yourself and get help.

- ✔ Learn to identify when your fears are pushing you toward an unhealthy focus on money. If you are able to spot these tendencies sooner, you will deal with them better. For example, let's say you're behind in your caseload performance, and it's eating at you. You're on your way to meet a donor, and your original intention was simply to cultivate the relationship. But the fear is rising up inside you. And a voice inside screams, "Get the money!" This is a perfect time to step out of the situation before you do any real damage. When these feelings well up, force yourself to wait before you take action.

- ✔ Make the right choice. After waiting, act wisely. In the example above, you might decide to get back to cultivation as you originally planned.

✔ Talk about this dynamic in your workplace by bringing up the topic of money vs. relationship. People will thank you. Remember to be kind and balanced in your approach. Be supportive, not demeaning, so you will be listened to and not ignored.

Money plays a very important role in our society and our workplace. Of course, it is a central item in major gifts fundraising. But the second you begin to value money over relationships, you start down a path of failure.

Pitfall 3.

Putting busy-ness over business. "Here comes the boss! Look busy!" We've all said it or thought it from time to time. At some point in our lives, most of us have worked in a boring job, hours pass, trying to look busy but getting very little done. Lack of motivation is a core reason many people stray from doing the right things.

But another reason we get off track is because we don't regularly pause to assess what we're doing. Try this: Look back over the previous thirty days and ask yourself, "Is this what I want to be doing with my time? Do the things I'm emphasizing get me closer to where I want to be, or are they pulling me farther away from it?"

Of course, these questions presume that you know where you want to be, and that's not always the case. If you've not done so recently, take some time to think about and write down your personal objectives. Regularly review them against how you use your time. Are you investing your time in tasks that will help you achieve your goals? It's easy to get off track, which is why you need to check it on a regular basis. You might find that you're always very, very busy yet you're wandering off course in one or more objectives. We humans have a strong tendency to pursue what's easiest, and not necessarily what's right. Over time, we often migrate away from what we're supposed to do.

One place where you might see evidence that you've gone off course is by comparing your job description to what you do every day. Often there will be a major discrepancy. Granted, the reason may be that your boss has asked you to take on these other tasks. But you may find that you've simply migrated toward those tasks you find easiest or least stressful. If you can, take a moment right now and pull out your job description and compare it to what you are doing today. Is it the same? If it's different, how much of what you're doing today is because your manager added the responsibility? How much is because you added things? Did either you or your manager decide you no longer needed to do certain things?

It takes massive discipline and time for leaders, managers and employees to stay focused on the right things. And what's true for individuals is equally true for organizations. It's easy for an entire organization to move from a place of being effective to simply being active. Just being busy is the first sign that an organization is on a track toward problems and failure.

You would think an annual planning process, if your organization has one, would take care of this. But it often doesn't— because even when trying to look at the "big picture," leaders and managers rarely stop to ask, "Are we doing the right things?" Instead, they're obsessed with getting the plan and budget accomplished.

An MGO needs to ask himself or herself two questions:

1. *"Am I doing the right things in my job?"* Stop and take an inventory now. Your primary responsibility might be to manage a qualified list of donors. Are you spending most of your time doing that—at least 80 percent of your time? Or are you doing other work that's taking you off this point? Examine why and get back on track.

2. "Am I doing the right things with my donors?" This is critical. It's easy to fall into a formulaic pattern in managing a donor or group of donors: You send the quarterly

newsletter, write or call from time to time, mail the project report, and occasionally visit in person. Maybe this is the right approach for a particular donor—but not necessarily. Engage your mind to ask, "Am I doing the right thing with this donor, or am I just following a major gifts formula and keeping busy?"

The most effective MGOs ask these questions constantly. They regularly go back to the baseline, imagining that they are looking the donor in the eye and asking, "What can I do for you? What can I do to fulfill your hopes for this great cause we're involved in?" Then, they set about doing it. These MGOs are often way more effective than those who aren't taking this inventory.

If you are the head of a nonprofit development program, encourage your MGOs to ask themselves these two questions every month. Or, if you're a major gifts officer, ask them of yourself. It's an exercise that will keep everyone on track.

It's difficult to stay on point when there are so many distractions. But it's so satisfying to reach the right destination. When it comes to the donors to whom you relate, there's nothing better than to have helped each of them find the right place in your organization.

Pitfall 4.

Putting overhead percentages over goals. Somewhere along the line, someone came up with the idea that nonprofits can and should operate their businesses in a substantially different way than a commercial company. Somehow, when it comes to nonprofits, office rent should be cheaper, highly talented employees should require less salaries, and good IT and HR departments are an unnecessary luxury. According to such thinking, nonprofits shouldn't need a sales force (like MGOs), nor should they seek to develop the same expert marketing, finance, operations and administrative departments as a successful commercial business. Where did this idea come from? It may be the misguided result of someone's attempt to make donors believe all their money goes directly to the cause.

But the more obsessed a charity is with minimizing its real or perceived overhead costs, the less obsessed it can be with changing the world.

Many nonprofits go out of their way to try to make it look as if virtually none of their money goes to overhead costs. Often, these "creative" accounting efforts amount to a nonprofit version of "cooking the books."

We all know that in the commercial world, "cooking the books" means presenting a company's financial records in the best possible light, even if it means falsifying them. So, you can understand why the executive director of a charity might be angered by the suggestion that something similar is going on.

But what can you say when you hear nonprofits claiming their overhead is 3 percent to 4 percent—or even 8 to 12 percent— when the facts tell a different story? The obsession with overhead percentages is interesting, because we've trained the giving public to believe that an extraordinarily low overhead is good—even when reducing it isn't practical and claiming to have achieved such percentages simply isn't true.

I (Richard) was at the board meeting of a major nonprofit, making a presentation on the marketing and fundraising plans we had created for them. There were some very successful business owners and CEOs sitting around the table. As I was making the presentation, the conversation wandered off into overhead. One of the business owners—a man who had started a very successful high-tech company—spoke up and said, "I'm very concerned about the overhead of this nonprofit. We really need to hold our overhead percentages at 12 percent."

I had anticipated this comment because I knew Larry (not his real name) and had been briefed about his concern about overhead. So, I jumped in and said, "Larry, I've been reading about your company. You are up to $600 million in revenue now, but I think you could be making more profit." He leaned forward, fully engaged, as I continued. "You should outsource your HR and IT functions, cut your sales force in half, reduce employee benefits by 10 percent..." I went on listing ideas that would have decimated his company by blindly cutting costs.

When I stopped, Larry shook his head and said, "Richard, I couldn't do any of those things." I responded, "Then why do you think this good organization can run on less than yours can?"

The fact is that this obsession with low overhead in the nonprofit world has run amok. There are thousands of nonprofits out there claiming their overhead is less than 10 percent, which is amazing. Even nonprofits that spend as little as 20 percent of their income on overhead often feel pressure to put more money toward programming. But is it really possible to successfully run an organization on that?

The nonprofit sector is working hard to maintain an outdated paradigm. The new generation of donors understands what it takes to run a successful business—whether it a corporation or a nonprofit. These donors are more concerned about impact than about overhead percentages. And that's where our attention should be. How many lives are we saving or impacting? How is our planet a better place because of our efforts?

We're not suggesting there should be no controls or standards for overhead. There are definitely scam artists out there who set up nonprofits simply to line their own pockets. There are also well-intentioned leaders who find themselves in situations where serious pruning needs to happen, and they lack the courage to do it. So, they may be inclined to play with the numbers to make them look better. Those leaders need to be disciplined and controlled by their board.

Thousands of nonprofits are doing fantastic work but are laboring under the false premise that overhead under 20 percent is the absolute standard for every well-run nonprofit. But organizations and leaders who keep obsessing on these percentages are forced to focus more on money, rather than on the cause they were founded to address. This puts those nonprofits on a path toward failure.

It's a delicate dance. Every organization needs to watch and manage its overhead. But impact must be the final objective. This is an important issue for fundraising, because those of us working in major gifts will have opportunities to discuss these concerns with donors and reason them out. Luckily, most donors who fully engage on this topic are reasonable and practical people. So, as you deal with the donors on your caseload, don't be afraid to focus your conversations on the difference their support is making and the impact your work is having—not on how little you're spending to do it.

Pitfall 5.

Putting power over effectiveness. We've already emphasized that effective nonprofits recognize that they are actually serving two parties: the people or cause the nonprofit is organized to benefit and the donors who support that effort. And we believe that half of a nonprofit's energy should be directed to its donors— rather than just tossing a few crumbs their way in exchange for their money.

But maybe we should add a third party to this mix of people your nonprofit serves: you and your colleagues—the people who actually work at the nonprofit. Having observed the management and leadership dynamics in many nonprofits, we can affirm that a lot of them already recognize this. But there are way too many other groups whose leaders, managers, and employees are more interested in position, power, and control than they are in effectiveness, service, and opportunity. What does this kind of dysfunctional environment look like?

- ▶ People focus on improving their standing in the organization rather than on getting meaningful work accomplished.
- ▶ Authority figures value their time more than the time of others.
- ▶ Critical thinking is actively discouraged.
- ▶ Certain "higher value" positions in the organization receive substantially better perks.

- Staff members are obsessed with "territory" in terms of job or influence.
- There's little interest in talking about impact, effectiveness, or new opportunities.
- Different work styles and approaches are not tolerated.
- Organizational structure is oriented toward control and hierarchy rather than participation.

And the list goes on. In essence, there's a high focus on self over others in such environments. This is amazing because the very essence of a nonprofit is to serve others—or at least it should be! Leo Tolstoy summed up this situation very succinctly: "Everybody thinks of changing humanity, but nobody thinks of changing himself."

Nonprofits can expend a great deal of energy and time talking about how they are going to change the world. But if nonprofit leaders are unwilling to look at themselves and their organizations and consider how they should change as well; this will creep into the way they treat donors. Supporters will be thought of as I.D. numbers and sources of cash rather than who they really are—beautiful human beings who give of their hearts and resources to help the charitable sector do something meaningful in the world. If you're in an organization where the focus is on power and control rather than effectiveness and opportunity, be careful. If you don't watch out, that same spirit will shape how you interact with your donors. That could look something like this:

- You're more concerned about how a donor can sustain your organization than about the good she can accomplish through her giving.
- You will value your time more than the time of your donors.
- You will find it difficult to listen to a donor's take on how your organization thinks and acts, missing important feedback.

- ▶ You'll find yourself impatient with any style or approach that is different from your own.
- ▶ You'll want to control how donors respond and react rather than allow them to fully participate.

Notice how the concern is all about you and what you want? That's a problem. You probably don't mean to be doing things this way. But the pressure of the work, the need to perform, and the culture of the organization may have taken you off track.

Awareness of these issues can help you counter any negative trends and sliding values shaping your work with your good donors. You want your relationship to donors to become focused on effectiveness and opportunity. This doesn't mean you have to abandon plans you already have in place. But it does mean:

- ▶ Finding information on how your programs are changing lives and the planet and sharing that information (and joy) with your donors, focusing especially on the parts of your work that interest them most.
- ▶ Spending all the time donors require so they can feel connected to the programs they're giving to.
- ▶ Showing more concern about the donor than yourself.
- ▶ Seeking answers to any question's donors have, even if those answers may be uncomfortable or probe into areas you'd rather not talk about. This will force you to be authentic.
- ▶ Processing ideas donors may have on how the organization can be more effective in its service.

There are many more ways to let donors into your world and to treat them with honor and respect. If you're in a place where power and control are valued more than effectiveness and opportunity, you may have to find your way out of the organization if things don't change. And remember, if the relationship with donors is off point, it's not the fault of your donors. They are doing the best they can, with good hearts and the best intentions.

Commit yourself, today and every day, to care for them in a very special way.

Pitfall 6:

Putting growth over greatness. Growth is exciting. Think about it. As a parent, it's incredibly exciting to watch your child grow and take on new challenges. If you're growing intellectually or emotionally, or moving forward in your career, that's a great thing. If your compensation is growing or you have a growing group of friends, why would you turn from that path? Growth is good. Growth shows progress. Growth means you are doing things right. Doesn't it? Yes—sometimes.

Many nonprofit directors seem obsessed with talking about growth. In a recent meeting with one director, he mentioned growth in every other sentence: "Our goal is to grow our grant income by 100 percent in the next three years." And, "We feel confident our supporters will be satisfied with the growth our organization has shown in the past six months." And, "Our board is very pleased with the progress we've made in revenue growth."

There's nothing wrong with those statements. But where are the people the nonprofit is serving? Why didn't he mention the cause the donors are giving to? Where's the passion for the need the nonprofit is organized to address?

"Oh, come on," you might be saying. "Give us a break. Certainly he talked about more than that?"

No, he didn't. The focus of the entire conversation was on growth, revenue, and organizational success—not about the results of the work. There was not a peep about the people or the cause! Sadly, that conversation seemed to reflect the heart of that leader—and such thinking surely shapes his board and staff, too. This individual's focus was on himself—his fame, standing, and achievements. It's a pretty sad state to be in, though it probably feels good for a season.

But that's just one person, right? Unfortunately, that's not the case. If you want to know how prevalent this focus is in the nonprofit sector, listen in on some conversations between non-profit leaders at your next fundraising conference. It may begin with the perfunctory, "Hi, Ralph, how are you doing?" But often the conversation proceeds something like this: "Doing great! Revenue is holding steady. Tough times, aren't they? How are you doing?"

Wouldn't it be great if the response to the "How are you doing?" question was, "I'm doing great! We helped 75 homeless people find a home and full-time employment this month!" Or, "Fantastic! We have helped to stop the spread of a debilitating disease among children in Malawi!" Or, "Couldn't be better. I've been encouraging our organization to listen more to our employees, donors, and board and take action on their ideas."

Former federal judge Sherman Finesilver once said, "Do not confuse notoriety and fame with greatness. For you see, greatness is a measure of one's spirit, not a result of one's rank in human affairs." The measure of one's spirit is not very sexy. It's hard to describe on a resume. True greatness and character aren't easy to summarize quickly. But when the leaders, managers, board, and employees of a nonprofit get hooked on the growth drug, it's easy to forget about being truly great.

Let's be clear: We are not against growth. But the path to true greatness is service—service to our cause, our donors, our colleagues, our organization, and our leaders; service to those we hold close and love, and even those we do not like.

Robert Kennedy said, "Few will have the greatness to bend history itself; but each of us can work to change a small portion of events, and in the total of all those acts will be written the history of this generation."

Consider how this attitude and approach could revolutionize the work you do:

- ▶ You move from seeking the money to helping donors achieve greatness through their giving.
- ▶ You move from competing with your colleagues to helping them become great.

- ▶ You move from laboring under the authority of your boss to helping him or her become successful.
- ▶ You move from an organizational culture focused on money and growth to one focused on the people or cause you serve.

Best of all, you maintain this attitude while being a top performer yourself. It's all about attitude, spirit, focus, and approach. It's about character and things of real value.

Most every reason why a nonprofit can fail has something to do with focusing on self over others. When leaders, managers, and employees become self-absorbed, both individually and as a group, failure is just around the corner. It might seem unlikely for nonprofits and the people who work in them to become self-obsessed, but it happens—again and again.

Become an agent of change in this area. Start with yourself, by pledging to be a person of service to others. Then, begin to quietly influence those around you, carefully and sensitively calling them to greatness.

Pause for Thought:
Beware of the Giant Hairball
Jeff Schreifels

The worst thing you can do as a major gift officer is to get involved in the Giant Hairball. It's a term coined by Gordon MacKenzie, in his book *Orbiting the Giant Hairball: A Corporate Fool's Guide to Surviving with Grace* (Viking 1996). He explains that essentially the Giant Hairball is anything in your organization—from procedures to possibilities, rules to radical ideas—that distracts you from your real work, which is knowing your donors, bringing them funding opportunities, and serving them outrageously.

Anything outside of that is getting tangled up in the Giant Hairball of your organization. If you're honest, you know exactly what we're talking about. How many times have you been asked to help out with an event or brainstorm a new program that has nothing to do with your donors? How many times do you look up at the clock from your desk and realize you've spent half your day doing paperwork and chatting with the planned-giving officer down the hall about one of his donors?

How about the time you wanted to help one of your donors fund his passion at your organization, and your organization said no because the program person didn't like the idea. You had to go back to your donor and tell him no because you let the Giant Hairball win.

It's hard not to get sucked into the Giant Hairball. It's actually enticing, and for some reason, MGOs seem to get sucked into it very easily.

When I sit down with an MGO, I will often ask him or her

to tell me about a particular donor they have on their caseload. Sometimes, in response to such a question, there's a long pause. And a look of worry. "Well, I really don't know that donor yet. I've only had him on my file for three months."

Three months and you don't know a key donor? There's really no excuse for this. But, when I ask why the MGO doesn't know the donor, the answer almost always is about the organization's Giant Hairball that has drawn them in.

I spoke with an MGO who told me she had a donor who was really interested and wanted to make a major gift, but he wanted to be creative about that gift. She went to leadership about that idea, and they put up a roadblock. And she left it at that. And that meant a lot of good work that might have gotten done just didn't happen.

So, let me be clear. Your job as the MGO is to orbit the Giant Hairball, not to let it run your life or get sucked into it.

The worst moment is when all of the organizational "goings on" pull you in. If you go in too far, you may never come out! If you feel yourself being drawn toward the Giant Hairball, take steps now to pull yourself out! Otherwise, you won't know your donors, you won't be able to come up with creative offers to put in front of them, and you won't be able to create amazing ways to steward them. Let your manager deal with the Giant Hairball. And, if you're a manager, do all you can to keep your MGOs from getting sucked into the Giant Hairball.

As an MGO, if you're getting pulled into the Giant Hairball, work creatively with your manager to find ways to escape its gravitational pull. The Giant Hairball wants you. But have confidence that you won't let it get you.

Chapter 6:
Setting Up for Success

"Well, we realized we needed a major gifts program—so we just started one."

Huh?

You hear this kind of talk all the time—from charity professionals who begin a major gifts program without careful planning. They think the money will just flow like water out of a tap.

In reality, if they're lucky, the money may start to drip in after a few years. And even that may not happen, unless they are asking themselves critical questions like:

- ▶ Does our structure ensure that the program can actually work?
- ▶ What kind of donors do we have?
- ▶ What do we need the money for?
- ▶ Do we have any major gift officers in the wings, and do they have experience?
- ▶ What program needs do we have that can help us create a compelling ask?
- ▶ Did we dedicate eight months to getting our major gifts officers up to speed?

The fact is, generating a sustainable major gifts program is a long and laborious process. Skipping steps will undermine your ability to raise money. Simply having a great cause and a good-hearted and even talented MGO doesn't mean you have the formula for automatic success. Starting and maintaining a good program takes discipline, thoughtfulness, strategy, and focus.

The Major Gift Value Triad

Whether you're working in an established major gifts program or just getting one started, there's always room for improvement. And that's a good thing!

We believe every successful major gift program must do three things. Keeping these three tasks in balance is essential. They are like the three legs on a stool. First, you need to raise significant dollars for a good cause. Second, you've got to retain donors. Third—and this is a crucial piece that's often neglected—you must consistently provide meaningful and fulfilling work for your MGO.

Maintaining ongoing relationships with donors and building meaning into a staff person's life might not feel like top priorities today. Getting the funding in right now is all-important, right? Well, yes, it's essential, but it's not the whole answer.

Retaining donors is often underemphasized. Most of the major gift files we see lose between 40 and 60 percent of their value each year. That means millions of dollars are simply vanishing into thin air. The economy isn't shrinking at that rate! What it actually means is that your donors are vanishing into thin air, or they're giving to—or spending on—something else. Raising funds immediately is essential, but maintaining your current donors is just as critical to your long-term sustainability.

It's pretty easy to see why retaining donors is essential. But here's the truth: Providing meaningful and fulfilling employment for your MGO simply can't be overlooked. If you're keeping donors and raising money but not offering your MGO work that he or she finds fulfilling, there's trouble ahead. With the tenure of most major gifts officers lasting just over two years, few managers in this field can say they're experts at stewarding this important human resource. And just as there's a direct connection between losing donors and losing dollars ... you guessed it—there's also a direct connection between losing MGOs and losing donors!

Here's another way to look at this and it is summed up in what we call the **Major Gift Value Triad**:

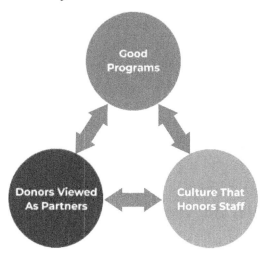

1. Your organization must have the ability to raise money, which is a by-product of doing good work and providing the donating public opportunities to engage with it;

2. You must have a deeply held belief that donors are partners in your work, not just sources of cash, which fosters a strong desire to nurture and retain them; and

3. You must have a business environment and culture that honors its staff and provides meaningful and fulfilling work.

If you're missing any of these essentials, don't read any more right now. Just start working on getting the entire Major Gift Value Triad established in your organization.

Building the Major Gift Pipeline

If we had a donor-centered view, our organization would be a place where everyone is working together for the common good of the **donor**—picture a line of department heads all holding hands with a single focus on the donor. They would be linked together as a chain, carefully, and with a caring spirit, passing the donor through the upgrading and retention process—always driven by the donor's passions and interests.

As we have thought about it at Veritus the entire fundraising effort—from acquisition all the way through to transformational giving—should not be viewed as individual rooms of the fundraising house or even as the classic pyramid, which also conceptualizes the fundraising process as one stacked upon another, but each still separate. Rather, we think the entire process should be viewed as a pipeline: a continuous, fluid flow that nurtures and cares for the journey of the donor.

The Major Gift Pipeline

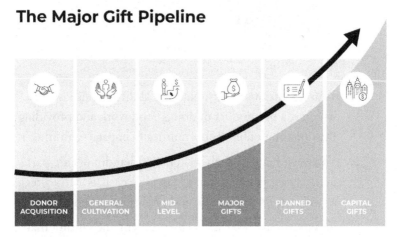

Think about this as it relates to one of your donors. They find out about your cause and are enticed by your offer to have them join your growing group of supporters. They join by giving their first gift.

But now they are cared for by a group of employees in your organization who regularly talk to each other about how that donor is doing in **their** journey with the organization. Questions are being asked. What else can we do for her? What more can we say about how her giving is making a difference? What does she care about? How can we serve that caring in a meaningful way? How can we carefully pass her along through the pipeline to greater involvement with us?

This kind of thinking transforms fundraising in two ways:

1. *It focuses first on a donor and her interests and passions.* Yes, this can be done through mass mailings, etc. Technology is now at the point where you can take your organization's budget and cause and create a **Donor Impact Portfolio** (DIP) see chapter 9 where all of your programs are placed into categories and subcategories—tracks, if you will—that the donor can come into (acquisition) and then journey on through (cultivation and upgrading) in her donor life with you.

2. *It creates strategies and systems to serve those passions and interests with an economic goal of helping donors give to their fullest capacity.* This is why we are reframing the fundraising process from how it is currently viewed to one that views the entire process as the major gift pipeline, i.e. helping the donor give to their capacity. Right now, we organize by giving level: mass market (the smaller givers), midlevel, major, planned, etc. Note that this is OUR view of donors, not their view of us. Think how powerful it would be if we organized our strategies and systems around our program categories and subcategories—individual interest and passion tracks, if you will, that the donor could run on. It would be powerful. Yes, we would still pay attention to giving levels for all the reasons we do now. But our focus and overall strategy would be different—creating and maintaining those individual program tracks that match donors' passions and interests.

At its simplest, the major gift pipeline is about: the concept that everything that happens in fundraising in an organization should be organized in a way that shepherds and cares for a donor, from the time they are brought into the organization all the way through their life with the organization.

Looking at it this way means that everything that happens with the donor is strategically and relationally knitted together to create a major gift pipeline since the end objective is to serve a donor's passions and interests in a manner that encourages them to give to their potential.

But very few leaders and managers in non-profits understand this dynamic. Instead, they create and manage the various functions as separate entities, each with their own performance metrics and net revenue expectations.

Now, that is not bad, in that the organization needs the net revenue each function delivers. But the problem is that hardly anyone is watching out for the individual donor's journey **through** the organization. And that results in a culture and environment where money is valued more than relationship.

When that happens, *donors literally run out of the organization or give less*—at rates sometimes as high as 60% of their value, year over year.

Why should you, as an MGO or major gift manager, care about this? Here are four things that will happen if you don't:

1. *You'll have fewer donors to cultivate* for major gift work, and the ones that remain will usually not be high-potential donors. Those donors have either already left your organization or are disillusioned and giving less.

2. *Your current caseload donors will be in an environment that is not donor-friendly,* meaning that you will need to be extra vigilant to make sure they are thanked and cared for promptly and properly.

3. *You will not have a robust reporting-back system in place* to tell your donor that her giving is making a difference.

4. *Your attempts to be donor-centered will have little support, since the focus is on getting the money rather than treating a donor as a full partner in your cause.*

Because of this, you won't be as successful as you could be. And by success, we mean two things: securing the revenue you need to fund your organization's programs and treating your caseload donors in a way that honors, respects and lifts them up.

What can you do about this? We have some suggestions:

▶ Start building and maintaining bridges between your work in major gifts and the other fundraising functions in the organization. Talk, share ideas, have a meal, hang out. Educate those you come in contact with about the major gift pipeline and how you all need to work together to steward the donor through it. This is probably the most important work you can do—to bring awareness.

▶ Talk to your manager about the pipeline and the need to have conversations and make plans that cross departments and fundraising functions. You may get a cold stare—or you may, surprisingly, find warm reception to the idea. After all, donors who are properly cared for will stay longer and give more. What's not to like about that?

Bringing awareness, asking questions and offering solutions on this topic will slowly bring change. And that will be good for your donors, for you, and for your organization.

Understanding the Place of Major Gifts

Every good major gifts program must have a clear understanding of the differences between major gifts and direct marketing, public relations, or events. Your organization's reporting structure should reflect the knowledge that major gifts is not direct marketing, although it may use some DM strategies; it is not public relations, although it will certainly seek to preserve and promote the organization's brand; and it is not events, though it may use events (very sparingly) to build relationships with caseload donors.

If major gifts isn't any of these things, then what is it? Major gifts fundraising is a one-to-one relationship where your sole aim is to match a donor's passions and interests to the goals of the organization. Too many nonprofits let other things get in the way of this, often because of the way they are structured. Perhaps the major gifts officer reports to the manager of direct marketing. Or, major gifts may be lumped together under one department along with public relations and events (sometimes to the point where an events manager is lead of the major gifts agenda).

If this is how your organization works, please don't be insulted when we say it's truly crazy. Such a structure is so incredibly harmful to a major gifts program that we have to wonder why some organizations function this way. The only thing we can conclude is that there's often a fundamental ignorance about what a major gifts program is and how it works. In some cases, there might be a bias toward some other marketing or communications effort that keeps the major gifts program subordinate to other agendas and objectives. But whatever the reason, such a situation is, frankly, a recipe for disaster.

Major gifts should be a function by itself, with the MGO reporting directly to the director or vice president of development. Major gifts might even be a department of one person. It shouldn't have PR, events, volunteer management, direct marketing, or any other manager laying out its plans. A major gifts program should be solely dedicated to managing, nurturing, upgrading, and relating to significant donors. That's it.

And who should be part of the major gift team? Professionals who relate to individual major donors, those who are in touch with foundations, gifted team members who handle corporations and businesses, and talent that relates to institutions like other nonprofits, churches, synagogues, parishes, social-service clubs, and other source of potential funding. All these types of major donor have one thing in common: They each require a one-to-one, personal approach. That's why you should include them in the major gift function. Everything else belongs somewhere else.

Unfortunately, this concept sounds like fundraising heresy to some nonprofit managers and leaders. Often, it only begins to make sense when these leaders realize that significant dollars are lost each year and hundreds, sometimes thousands, of donors are disappearing.

Shepherding donors is a sacred trust, a mysterious and mystical responsibility to be valued and treasured. Believe this, and then take steps to align your organization so that it can properly and effectively house an effective major gifts program.

Bare Essentials Checklist

Here's a brief checklist of the essentials for starting and maintaining a major gifts program. There's a lot of detail related to each of these points (some of which we touch on later in this chapter and through the second half of the book). But here are the highlights:

☑ **1. Design the right organizational home for major gifts.** As we've just emphasized, major gifts is not direct marketing, public relations, or anything else. We often see managers place the entire major gifts program under the direct-marketing manager. Big mistake. Don't do it. Major gifts should have a direct relationship to the director of development.

☑ **2. Create the right job description.** Whether you're looking to improve the performance of your current major gifts program or seeking a new team member to slot into your organization, creating the ideal job description is critical. Often, we find that job descriptions for major gifts officers are poorly written and provide little direction! And then everyone wonders why the major gifts officer is failing. (We'll talk more about writing an effective job description later in this chapter.)

☑ **3. Find and hire the right people.** This is one of those things that just needs to be right. We also have a checklist for the minimums in this area. Get this step wrong, and you will have dark days ahead. Get it right, and you're in for a thrilling time.

☑ **4. Select the right donors.** Every donor is different. Just because a donor reaches a certain level of giving does not mean that donor should always be assigned to an MGO. Major gifts work is built around making personal one-to-one connections with donors who desire such relationships. But a person may give a massive amount but may not want to put their arm around your MGO. We'll talk more about how to qualify the right donors for an MGO caseload in part two.

☑ **5. Segment major donors into top-, middle- and lower-giving potential.** Also, select three to five of the top-tier donors with whom you will spend a great deal of time and to whom you'll submit major proposals.

☑ **6. Set goals and make plans for every donor.** What? Make plans for them? Yes. If you don't know where your organization is going strategically and financially, you won't get there. Make plans that include your donors, which means being sure that a critical part of your work is to identify and serve their passions and interests.

☑ **7. Develop offers.** Work with finance and program to come up with significant and substantial offers you can present to major donors.

☑ **8. Identify Outcomes.** Work with program to come up with a believable outcome for the programs and projects you are presenting to donors. Donors need to know their giving is making a difference.

☑ **9. Produce monthly donor reports.** Such reports should capture how the same donors are performing month to month and year to year. They should measure progress against goals. These reports will tell everyone how the MGO is performing and give management an idea of return on investment. Sound scary? Perhaps. But we're all rated on performance. When it's acknowledged, good performance inspires even better.

☑ **10. Have a process for integrating new donors.** Not all donors currently on an MGO's caseload will perform as expected, and surprising new donors will migrate up to major-donor level through direct marketing. You need to plan for this dynamic. Cooperate in this area; don't compete.

☑ **11. Keep focused on the big picture.** Make sure the case-load value is growing, the MGO is productive, and sufficient funds are being raised for the organization. Don't say "oops" and ignore it. Expect this program to be successful, and work hard.

Now, if you do all of this—with discipline, thoroughness, and focus—your major gifts program will be successful. Sounds simple, doesn't it? Actually, it is! But here's the rub. If you aren't diligent, you won't execute all these points. You'll take a shortcut here and cut corners there. You'll give priority to other urgent and seemingly more important tasks, and you'll soon find yourself wandering off-course. And that's where it all starts to fall apart. So be vigilant in all of these areas. Do them with excellence, energy, and excitement. You'll be really happy with the result.

The Job Description

Some job descriptions require the MGO to do administrative work, public relations, communications, and a host of other informational and marketing tasks. Often, such job descriptions say almost nothing about fundraising, let alone a caseload of donors. When writing an MGO job description, think on the values and priorities that should be represented in each section. Consider these specifics:

✔ **Job title:** You may want to have two titles: an internal title for HR and management purposes, and a public title that is used in relations to donors. The internal title is the functional, organizational position, like major gifts officer. The public title should never mention money or fundraising. Think "Donor-Relations Director," because it emphasizes the people who support your programs.

- ✔ **Staff member to whom the position reports:** This should be only one person. Don't pull a major gifts officer in two different directions.
- ✔ **Other staff who relates closely with the role:** These are mostly other MGOs, program people, and finance. Don't include PR, marketing, or communications in here.
- ✔ **Purpose of the position:** State this very simply and directly: "To secure funds for the organization by managing a caseload of assigned donors, assuring that as many as possible are retained as donors and upgraded in their giving and involvement." There are several key values in this purpose statement. The primary focus is to secure funds—not make impressions, deal with volunteers, or be a community activist. It's about raising money from an assigned group of donors, and retaining and upgrading them.
- ✔ **Office hours and travel:** A job description must establish expectations regarding travel and time away from the office. Far too many major gifts officers expect to stay at home most of the time. But the MGO's primary work is to connect with donors outside the office. This needs to be clear.
- ✔ **Benefits of the position:** It's important to tell the employee or prospective employee how the job will benefit him or her. Try this: "The benefit of this position will be the satisfaction of helping donors fulfill their passions and interests through their giving to (name of organization)." Notice that this doesn't mention money. It's about helping the donors realize their interests and passions. This is important.
- ✔ **Ongoing responsibilities:** Try to limit the categories of work to no more than five specifics, along with a required catch-all category:
    - Will qualify a group of caseload donors.
    - Will create individual goals for each donor based on the donor's history of giving and knowledge of that donor's potential.

- Will create a plan for each donor on the caseload that will serve as the foundational communication and marketing plan for that individual. Will execute such plans faithfully and in a timely manner so that individuals on the caseload are retained and upgraded.

- Will work with the program and communications departments to secure appropriate project information (including budgets), and create offers, proposals, and asks that will be used with persons on the caseload to secure gifts.

- Will create monthly reports that accurately reflect caseload activity and performance.

- Will perform other major-donor activities as required.

✔ **Accountability and measurements of performance:** This mirrors the role responsibilities. For every responsibility required, you must state a measurement of it. Many MGOs wonder how they'll be evaluated. Here's how:

- Ability to qualify donors who represent the highest giving potential for the organization.

- Ability to create reasonable financial goals for each donor based on their past giving and potential.

- Ability to create a personal contact and ask plan for each donor that takes into account the individual donor's interest, motivations, giving patterns and ask preferences.

- Ability to execute the plan for each donor on the caseload, in a timely and cost-effective manner, so that donors can be retained and upgraded.

- Ability to secure project and organization information and create and write effective offers, proposals, and asks.

- Ability to secure information that can be sent back to donors to report on how their money was used.

- Ability to create timely reports that reflect caseload and MGO performance.

- Ability to manage people, process, deadlines, and budget while adhering to the policies and procedures of the organization.
- Ability to get along with peers, subordinates, and management, and maintain a positive and constructive attitude while solving problems.
- Ability to protect the mission, goals, and values of the organization.

This list summarizes a range of values important to every employee of any organization, and caps off the ideal major gifts officer job description. It states succinctly how the major gifts officer will be evaluated, and also sets clear expectations for performance and attitude.

Be very diligent about writing good job descriptions for each major gifts officer. It's essential that these good people know what they're supposed to do, and know how they will be evaluated. It's so tragic to see so much fulfillment and joy lost on something that only takes a few minutes of clear and straightforward thinking.

Six Surprising Attributes of Extraordinary MGOs

Looking for talent to fill that role? Or perhaps you're trying to develop your own skills as a major gifts officer. Keep an eye out for individuals who consistently demonstrate these six counterintuitive behaviors—or foster them in yourself.

1. Extraordinary MGOs set goals they can't reach. If setting unreachable goals sounds like setting yourself up for failure, think again. Some MGOs occasionally resort to sandbagging, which means they never aim for any goal they might not achieve. This makes their numbers easy to reach and even overshoot.

Such MGOs may be able to surpass the goals they've set without actually working all that hard. But we believe that's setting yourself up for failure, because it sets mediocrity as the standard. Also, any good manager will spot such attempts.

It's understandable that you don't want to set an impossible target. Your stress will go through the roof as management expectations shoot up. Not a good idea. But here's a little trick. Set a goal with your manager—one that's reasonable, that you should be able to achieve with hard work. Be sure you're not sandbagging. Put a healthy percentage increase on top of last year's income. Then set a top-secret, private goal. Tell one other person, so you have some sense of accountability. But don't let your manager in on the secret. If you're a manager seeking to improve the performance of your MGOs, give them permission to do this—encourage them to seek that personal best.

Think hard about that secret goal. What could you achieve from your caseload if you really kicked it up a notch? This is where you say to yourself, "If I spent more time with these ten donors and worked up a proposal that really matched their passions, I could get them to do much more than even they think is possible." Thinking like this is a great internal motivator that really helps you stretch yourself. Even better, when you set that higher goal, more often than not, you will reach it.

While everyone else is gazing at the motivational posters hanging on their walls, you'll have your own very personal goal driving you forward. You'll be amazed at what happens when you actually put something down on paper and commit to it.

2. Embrace rejection. The best MGOs are pretty fearless in the face of rejection. Rejections are an indication that they're out there doing the work. MGOs who fear rejection should really be more afraid of unemployment. Those who fear rejection often exhibit some of the following behaviors:

- ✔ They research a donor to death, sometimes taking more than a year before even setting up a meeting. Research is paramount to really understanding a donor, but it can also become a barrier that prevents you from getting out there and asking.
- ✔ They spend all their time seeking new prospects and attending events. They may have a full caseload of qualified

donors, but instead of working with them, they devote all their attention to looking for new donors. Then they wonder why half the donors on their current caseload didn't give that year.

✔ They stay at their desks. Major gifts officers who fear rejection spend most of their time in the office writing up strategic plans and goals, and then reviewing them. Plans and goals are great, but the heart of major donor involves putting the paper down and facing real people. Sixty to seventy-five percent of your time should be spent talking to your donors, listening to them, and asking.

✔ They often complain that a donor meeting was canceled. After three or four cancellations, their bosses should begin to wonder if a meeting was ever scheduled in the first place.

✔ They're often explaining why they didn't meet their revenue goals that month. (Usually the answer has something to do with donors cancelling meetings.)

Extraordinary MGOs don't fear rejection. That doesn't mean they like rejection, but they know it's part of the territory. They know that the more they ask, the higher the likelihood that someone will say yes. That's how they view their work and their caseloads.

It's kind of like a professional baseball player. A great hitter fails seven out of ten times at bat. Even in his best-ever year, Ted Williams failed six out of every ten at bats. You don't have to succeed 100 percent of the time. Not even 50 percent of the time. A success rate of 40 percent can make you a hero.

Extraordinary MGOs know it's not about arranging the perfect meeting. It's about taking every chance to step up to the plate and ask, seeking to create matches between a donor's passions and the mission of the organization. Will there be rejection? Of course! But again, like a good hitter, extraordinary MGOs learn from those rejections, ask good "why" questions, and then get back out there and do it better the next time. Or, even if they don't do it better, they just keep at it with equal effort—and the next time the formula works.

3. Make mistakes. A common characteristic of extraordinary MGOs is that they make tons of mistakes. You might be thinking this doesn't make sense. If they were really good, they wouldn't make mistakes, right? Wrong! Think of the most respected political figures in history. They might look invulnerable on first glance, but dig a bit more deeply and you'll probably find they have made colossal errors and have experienced significant failures. But at other times, they got it right in a very big way.

Extraordinary MGOs are not afraid to try new things, to go out on a limb, to test unconventional ideas and strategies, and to do everything they can for their donors. The MGO who aggressively tries new strategies will make mistakes precisely because the strategies are untried. But these MGOs are extraordinary because they learn something new each time and rarely repeat the same error twice.

4. Ignore traditional timekeeping. If you sit down with extraordinary MGOs and ask them to tell you stories about a gift they helped secure or about how they cultivate and nurture their donors, you will find that they don't think of their jobs as something accomplished between the hours of 9 and 5. Instead, they view their jobs as a life passion, and schedule their time around their donors' needs.

If you are fortunate enough to be the manager of an extraordinary MGO, the worst thing you can do is to require that she punch the clock and work from the office every day. Too often, great MGOs have their spirits and creativity crushed by out-of- touch managers who think they need to be in the office everyday. Extraordinary MGOs do their most productive work by fitting in with donors' schedules. If a donor says, "I know it's late, but can you meet me at a diner at 10:00 p.m.?" there's little hesitation. If the only meeting an MGO can get is right before the donor's tee time on Saturday morning, the MGO makes sure she is at that meeting.

We met recently with an MGO who spoke of his frustration about his manager's insistence that he always work "regular hours" from the main office. "Most of my work as an MGO involves donor visits that are either in the evenings, at early mornings for breakfast, or on the weekends," he told us. "Yet I'm still required to be in the office by 8:30 every morning." When we sat down with his manager to review goals vs. actual revenue, we discovered that this MGO had surpassed his targets by double, year after year. Why would a manager require standard office hours from such a top performer? That's a big mistake. In fact, if you manage an MGO who always arrives at the office on time and leaves at 5:00 p.m. every day, you should probably be really concerned!

Extraordinary MGOs are less concerned with a forty-hour week than with getting to know their donors, deepening relationships, creating great offers to present for funding, and being both restless and relentless.

5. Don't have all the answers. One amazing quality of extraordinary MGOs is that they don't have all the answers. They know having all the answers isn't even possible. Instead, they demonstrate curiosity about everything, and this helps them find solutions to just about anything.

Less creative MGOs often get stuck behind roadblocks. They don't know what to do about a certain situation or donor—so they often allow months, even years, to go by without working out a solution.

Curiosity is a powerful tool because it can drive you to solve a problem. Curiosity leads to asking the question that creates the basis for understanding a donor and can catapult you to some very complex situations. Quite frankly, if you're not a curious, searching person you really should not be a major gifts officer.

Extraordinary MGOs don't get stuck for long. They thrive on figuring out how to get something done that might at first seem impossible. They love learning new things. They love getting to know more about the people they meet. They're interesting people. If you have dinner or lunch with an extraordinary MGO, you feel great at the end of the meal because he or she is interested in you. In fact, extraordinary MGOs are interested in everything.

 6. Never get comfortable. We believe the ideal caseload for an MGO includes 150 qualified donors. (More on this in part 2.) But among those 150 qualified donors, you will always have at least a dozen different situations that are problematic, complex, or difficult to solve. If you're doing your work well, you'll continually be hustling and working out solutions to problems. Challenging? Yes. Rewarding? Hugely. Fun? Often. But it's rarely comfortable.

 At meetings with MGOs, it's easy to tell who's extraordinary and who isn't by how fast the meetings seem to go. Meetings with extraordinary MGOs fly by because they're either super-animated as they discuss situations with their donors, or they're creatively brainstorming complex projects that have many twists and turns through which to navigate.

 If you're setting high goals, actively cultivating gifts from at least 20 percent of your caseload at all times, and carefully stewarding the other 80 percent, you'll naturally run into a number of situations that will be demanding and difficult. But being an MGO isn't supposed to be easy. It's not just sitting behind a walnut desk writing thank-you notes on fine paper. This is a job that requires you to be out there, going to any length for your donors and for your organization.

Understanding Failure, So You Can Avoid It

 Most of the failures in the major gifts business can be boiled down to a few basic issues.

 Sometimes the organization itself is a major reason an MGO's efforts are unsuccessful. Either the organization just doesn't have the program to present to donors or, if it does, it hasn't been prepared, packaged, and priced as it should be.

There are also cases where an MGO really doesn't belong in the job. He or she lacks either the talent or the burning desire to do the job well.

But in many cases, both the organization and the MGO are capable of success. And in these situations, MGOs who fail often do so simply because they aren't doing the job properly. It usually comes down to one or more of the following six factors.

▶ **Failure to understand the joy of giving.** It bears repeating that if you think fundraising is ultimately only about the money, you will fail. If this concept still feels surprising to you, then either we haven't been doing our job, or you haven't been reading very closely. You may want to flip back to the first chapter and start over.

▶ **Failure to have passion and vision for the organization.** If you don't really care about the cause of the organization you're working for, or if you think of your job as all about a paycheck, you will not succeed. You have to have passion for the cause. You need to have positive energy and be excited about the work your group is doing.

▶ **Failure to listen to and understand donors and put their interests first.** Too often, an MGO is so focused on getting the money (first mistake) that he doesn't listen to donors (second mistake) and, therefore, doesn't know their interests or how to serve them (the final, fatal mistake). It's about the donor.

▶ **Failure to understand the concept of moves management.** Moves management is a fancy term for relationship building. We use moves management when we're dating or courting; when we're looking for a job; whenever we want something and it requires finesse and influence. But for some reason many MGOs don't realize that they need to use these same skills in building relationships with donors. MGOs have to make those moves that help to cultivate and build these relationships over time.

- ▶ **Failure to ask.** Even many bold and assertive MGOs will sometimes back away from making the actual request for funding, forgetting that the act of giving is a real joy for donors. Some MGOs do everything right—except for making the ask! It happens more than you might think. And it's probably happened to you.
- ▶ **Failure to manage time and priorities effectively.** One of the questions we ask MGOs most frequently is, "Why did you do that?" Usually, the issue involves MGOS who spend too much time with less valuable donors, or who keep busy with non-caseload activity like attending conferences, or who sit in the office when they should be out meeting donors.

If you feel you're in the right job and working for the right organization, yet you're still experiencing failure, it's likely you're falling into one or more of these traps. So, take a close look at these six reasons for failure, and ask yourself if they apply to your situation. If any of them pertain to you, take steps to correct them. Just make a decision to address these issues, and you will get to a happier place.

Part 2:
Building Your Major gifts Program

Chapter 7:
The Seven Pillars of Major Gift Strategy

Have you seen the Academy Award-nominated film *Moneyball*? Sure, it's a film about a baseball team—but it's also about going against conventional wisdom and trying something new that nobody thinks has real merit, until it actually works! It's the story about the importance of having a vision for what you want to accomplish, and a plan for how you'll get there.

Back in our Domain Group days, when much of our work was focused on helping nonprofits build more effective direct-response programs, planning was a non-negotiable. Every team had at least a twelve-month plan. Every plan was filled with action steps, and every step had a specific date attached to it. Attached to the plan was a budget and pro forma of what we expected each action to cost, and how well it would perform.

Clients loved it because they knew exactly what was going to happen. The organizations we worked with used these plans to hold us—and themselves—accountable to what we had agreed to do together.

Today, our work is focused primarily on major gifts, but we still use the same discipline of planning today with our current clients. But here's the funny thing: Many of the major gifts programs we audit and review have nowhere near the same level of planning, discipline, focus, and accountability as their counterparts in direct response. Yet the major gifts program is very often responsible for the majority of the revenue.

Why on earth would an organization neglect the planning, discipline, budgeting, forecasting, and accountability aspects of this crucial program? Perhaps it's because work in major gifts involves dealing with individuals—and you think having a strategic plan is presumptuous when you're building relationships? Maybe you think that somehow it needs to be more natural and organic?

Whatever reasons you might have for not planning in major gifts, you've got to get over them—now. Creating a strategic plan for every donor in your major gifts programs is absolutely critical to your overall success. Here's why:

- ▶ *It gives you a road map that shows you where you're going.* If you allow your interactions with individual donors to be subject to the ebb and flow of your day or week, you will wander in your relationship to those donors. And that wandering will cause failure.
- ▶ *It provides a structure to work within.* This doesn't mean you can't change the plan as needed. In fact, a framework actually frees you to be more creative in the type of tactics you employ during the course of the year. Without a framework, you're simply scrambling.
- ▶ *It will impress your manager and colleagues.* If you present a full-year plan for every one of your donors with revenue goals attached and month-by-month cash-flow projections, they'll look at you with new respect.
- ▶ *It keeps you accountable.* Having specific plans and goals to reach with each donor guides you toward your bigger goal. Each donor strategic plan is a stepping stone on the path to providing robust revenue for your organization. It can only do you good.

► *It works!* Everyone in the major gifts world seems to be looking for the one big donor, the right mix of board members, or the magical campaign or event that will take their organization to the next level. Experience tells us that what actually works is staying focused on your donors, having a plan for each donor and working that plan, and remaining accountable. It's not sexy, but it's the foundation of most successful major gifts programs.

You may be asking: "What are the key components of major gift planning?" We think it involves the following seven steps or pillars which, when followed, will make you a successful major gift fundraiser.

In this chapter we will list the seven pillars and offer a short explanation of each one, to help you see how they fit together. Then, in the next several chapters, we will spend more time looking at what goes into each of these pillars so you can clearly understand what needs to be done in each of them and how they can help you build the right strategy for your major gifts program.

Pillar 1: Cultivate the Right Donors

If you hope to be successful in cultivating major donors, it's essential to make wise choices about which donors you will relate to. The most important thing is to choose a caseload of donors who WANT a deeper relationship with your organization.

But, as we've already indicated, it is also essential for every MGO to have a manageable number of donors on his or her caseload. This means each MGO is cultivating no more than 150 major donors. In addition, once you have qualified a group of no more than 150 donors, the donors should be grouped into three tiers (A, B, and C) based on your assessment of their ability and interest in giving. MGOs should expect to spend half of their time working with A-level donors.

In chapter 8, we will focus on how to do this effectively.

Pillar 2:
Establish a Revenue Goal for Every Donor

We strongly believe you need to establish a revenue goal for every donor on your caseload. This goal gives you a destination that can shape your work with each donor. The goal for each donor needs to be realistic, yet it should have a bit of a stretch in it as well. Why? Because these goals will help push you to new heights. In our experience MGOs that create goals with some stretch in them usually make them.

Often, we find that MGOs are reluctant to create goals for individual donors because they fear they will be reprimanded or may even lose their jobs if they don't make the goal. This is not what goals are about. Goals are there to 1) drive the plan for your donor; 2) help your team budget for the year; and 3) help you stay focused on the process to get to your goal.

Frankly, major gifts are often volatile. The changing circumstances of just one donor could totally "blow" all your goals for that year. Does that mean you have failed? Of course not. Not if you stayed with your process and plan. That truly is all you can control. But we have found that an MGO who creates a plan and stays focused on it will normally make or exceed their original goals.

Sometimes, MGOs are required to establish goals that are not their own—often such goals are just "what the boss wants." Or they may be told that giving needs to be raised a certain percentage, so they simply attach the same percentage of increase next to each donor's name. That's insanity. The goal for every individual donor should have a story that includes what he gave last year, his current financial situation, how he feels about your organization, and where you stand in relationship with him. It's not just assigning a dollar figure based on a previous dollar figure.

Pillar 3: Create a Strategic Plan for Every Donor

To put it simply, the strategic plan answers the question of how you're going to make your goals. Planning for every donor on your caseload is no small task. It means undertaking the arduous exercise of evaluating your interactions with that donor during the past year and analyzing the outcomes. It means thinking carefully about the type and timing of your communications, and how they relate to what your organization is seeking to do in the next year. It means creating a cash flow for your revenue goals that includes your best estimates for when the gifts will come in. And, of course, it requires really understanding each donor, so that you can effectively connect her passions with the good work you are doing.

Sometimes we talk with development officers who believe they do not need an individual plan for each donor because "My major donors just want to help." Of course, your major donors want to help. So do all the other people who support your organization. But does this mean all your supporters are exactly the same? If an individual shows noticeably greater inclination and capacity to give than most others, do you think she's letting you know she wants the exact same information and engagement as everyone else?

Successful major gifts programs are led by strategy, and this strategy means creating an individual moves management plan for each donor. It's only right that your contact with them should reflect their interests and make it clear that you know they're special.

Pillar 4: Ask Donors for Support

When the average person thinks of development or fundraising, "the ask" is what usually comes to mind first. Of course, asking for financial support is a key part of any good major gifts program. But too many nonprofits jump too quickly to that point without the necessary preparations and planning. If you've read this far, you know we view that as a major problem in many major gifts programs.

It is essential to match the hopes, dreams, and desires of your donors with the elements of your program. You can only do this if you are looking your donors in the eye and understanding exactly what programs or projects you have that will meet those desires and dreams. This means spending significant time with your donors, time that allows you to find out who they are, why they give, what they are most passionate about, and what elements of your organization's work will most interest them. Only then can you ask for their support in ways that are both effective and respectful.

A good ask builds a bridge between the passions and interests of the donor and the needs of the organization. Too many MGOs jump right into the process of writing proposals, thinking only about the needs of their organization. But unless your re- quest is based on knowing what a donor wants, he or she won't fully engage. In chapter 9, we will explore strategies to make your funding requests as personalized and effective as possible.

Pillar 5: Thank Donors

You might think we would not need to mention this; unfortunately, this key step is still too often neglected. Whenever we work with an organization, we spend some time talking to their donors to get a sense of their experiences. It's astounding how often they tell us that they never get thanked for their gifts. And, we're not talking about gifts of $10 or $25—we're talking about gifts of $10,000 or $25,000!

It is absolutely essential that you have this thanking business down. This means having a protocol in place to 1) send a receipt quickly (within 1 week of receiving the gift); 2) calling the donor within 3 days of receiving the gift and 3) if appropriate, have the executive director call to thank the donor.

Thanking every donor is an essential way of telling the people who support your work that you value them and their gifts.

You must not mess this up. It's key to a long relationship.

Pillar 6: Report Back

In surveys with donors asking why they stop giving to organizations, repeatedly the top answer is "I never heard back from the organization about how my gift made a difference." Sadly, we have found that many organizations have no process for making sure donors ever hear about the progress that has been made because of their support.

When donors make a substantial gift (or even a small gift) in support of a particular program or campaign, it is essential that you offer them updates on the progress of that program. You simply must make reporting back to donors a priority for your organization. Otherwise, you will always struggle with donor retention— and that will limit the good work you're able to do.

Donors need to know that their gifts make a difference. It's pretty simple: If you don't tell donors what their gift has helped to accomplish, you probably won't get another gift.

Pillar 7: Be Accountable

Accountability seems like a harsh word. For those of us who are independent spirits, the word can evoke negative feelings. This is too bad. Because accountability is a good thing. It helps us do what all of us—managers and employees, donors and staff—want to do.

But often, nonprofits don't have their act together on the accountability thing. Internally, the problem often starts with managers who do not define anything for their employees. An employee is hired to do a job, but everything about that job—including the job description and the objectives—is so vague that no one has a clear and common understanding of what needs to be done.

Unfortunately, in many nonprofits there seems to be little value placed on setting goals, measuring progress against those goals, and holding people accountable to do good and effective work. Good folks often struggle to help people or change the world through really good programs but often are stymied while money is lost, labor is wasted, laziness is rewarded, and a lot of mindless activity is being tolerated. Organizations spiral down because employees who want to do good work get the nagging feeling that there's a gap between what's expected of them and what they can actually deliver. That gap—such a nasty little gap—is what will tear them down.

When you go through those "dry" periods, someone has to be able to look you in the eye and say, "Hang in there, and trust the process. The process works." Such accountability will help you stay focused and prevent you from veering off into the woods and getting lost.

Accountability is not something punitive and negative—although many managers use it that way. Management and accountability systems and processes should be a kind, honest, direct way of helping a person meet expectations—not just management expectations, but their own expectations as well as those of their peers and subordinates.

Without good management and accountability, leaders will not lead as they should, MGOs will not perform as they should, and the funds for program will not come in as they should. But when management and accountability are done well, it's beautiful, because every person on the team is clear about expectation and has a chance to meet them. When managers do this kindly and positively, they will have happy, effective, and productive MGOs. Happy, effective, and productive MGOs mean happy donors. Happy donors mean programs receive funding, which is what we all set out to do in the first place.

So there you have it: *The Seven Pillars of Major Gift Strategy*. In the next three chapters we'll be exploring more details related to each of these pillars, so you can build a major gifts program that gets big results. We'll start in the next chapter by looking more closely at how to create the perfect donor pool and then develop financial goals and individualized plans for each donor.

Chapter 8:
Create the Perfect Donor Pool

Have you heard the terms *knighting* and *inviting*? You probably know of organizations that create "clubs" for donors in their regular communications stream, like a President's Circle or Monthly Partners. The direct-mail fundraiser will often invite donors to take up the challenge to give monthly, but then will "knight" higher-level donors into a special group as a means of thanks and recognition.

But charities often make the mistake of knighting donors into their major gifts programs when they should be inviting them. This typically happens to a donor who has a fairly long history of giving $50 here or $100 there in response to regular mail or e-appeals. Then she suddenly gives a big check for $1,000 or $5,000— and is immediately taken out of the regular donor communication stream and put into an MGO's caseload just because she passed the minimum-donation threshold.

In the normal donor communication stream, she had been receiving and responding well to 15 to 22 asks every year. Major donors often get only two or three asks. Also, the person who is now in charge of cultivating this "new" major donor may overlook her because she's often coming in at the lowest tier. Often, the MGO has bigger fish to fry. So in the majority of cases where a donor is handled this way, her giving actually goes down.

That's why it's so important to qualify a donor before introducing him to a major gifts program. By qualify, we mean that every donor added to a major gifts program meets three criteria: 1) The donor has the capacity (ability) to give; 2) the donor is a current supporter; and 3) the MGO has verified that the donor wants to relate to the organization in this way. A donor who has been qualified has done more than just given a certain size donation; he has responded to an invitation saying, "Yes, I'd be happy to receive personal attention from an individual."

The fact that a donor's gift meets a certain donation level or wealth capacity benchmark is not necessarily an indicator that he wants to be part of a major gifts program or desires to relate to you on a personal basis. In fact, most donors who give over a certain amount actually don't want to be part of a major gifts program. In our experience, only one in three donors whose giving has crossed the major-donor threshold actually want to relate more personally. This means that two out of every three donors on the average MGO's caseload are actually not interested in the kind of personalized attention that a good major gift program provides. These donors don't really want to talk. What a waste of time. And what an intrusion on an exceptional donor!

When you fail to qualify major gifts donors properly, you end up with a lot of donors on a caseload who become less engaged with your organization, reduce their giving, or even stop giving entirely. This is a major reason behind donor attrition: Many MGO's caseloads are packed with donors who want no part of it. This can feel hugely disheartening, but there's a clear remedy. Stated simply, you need to qualify donors before adding them to a caseload.

When you establish a caseload of qualified donors who are eager to learn more face to face, you have donors you can really work with. They're on board, and they've said so. And, if you qualify them carefully, you'll learn all kinds of information about them, which will help you honor and serve them in the future. And what happens when a person feels honored? Trust develops.

If you use dollar amounts as your only indicator of whether someone qualifies to be in your major-donor program, you're treating that person like a bag of cash. When someone gives an exceptional amount, make an exceptional effort to find out whether she would enjoy learning more from you in person.

Make Sure You Have the Facts About the Donor

Before you decide to make that exceptional effort, make sure you have the facts. What do you already know to be true about this donor and her interest in your organization? What is real? What do you know for a fact, and what are you assuming about the donor? If you're not sure about something, can you find out more before you start? Is there any question you need to be asking that goes below all the information you can gather on the surface?

It's essential to ask—and answer—these questions before you jump into action. In major gifts, we get so focused on getting the money and reaching management's goals that we hardly stop to think about what prospects we should really be pursuing.

Analysis is a major driver in selecting donors to be on your caseload and forecasting their performance. We suggest that it is ideal to have about 150 qualified donors on one caseload. Given what we've said about the percentage of donors who are likely to desire one-on-one interaction with the MGO, this means you'll need at least 450 candidates from your donor file to consider in your qualifying process.

But how do you know which donors to consider? Here's how to get the facts:

1. Look at your donor files and find those donors who have consistently given $1,000 or more cumulatively over recent calendar years. Remember, donors think in calendar years, not fiscal years. Look at the current year plus three past years.

2. Pair that information with available data regarding a donor's wealth or assets so you have a good picture of both current giving (inclination) and capacity.
3. Organize this information by types of donors: individuals, foundations, corporations, businesses, and other organizations.
4. Choose donors with high capacity who have recently given large gifts.
5. Keep an eye on recently lapsed high givers who have high capacity.
6. Put all those donors who have the highest recent giving, plus high capacity, onto your caseload pool list.
7. Put this list through a qualifying process to arrive at your qualified pool.

This is how you establish who should be on your caseload pool to qualify. Then, once you have a qualified caseload, do this same analysis on a monthly basis to keep an eye on how the donors are performing and what additional steps you should take in managing the caseload. Notice that this whole process involves continually crunching the data to uncover what's happening with donors. This lets the facts be your guide to action and planning.

To be sure, all of this analysis is complex and takes time. But it's an important pillar for success in major gifts fundraising. Maybe you've heard it said that, "Facts are friendly." They are. But facts are sometimes hard to come by. They're just like good friends! Pursue them with discipline and energy, and you will find that they truly are the friends people say they are.

Qualify the Right Number of Donors

When you meet someone for the first time, do you immediately consider that person to be a close friend? Of course not. Friendships take time to develop. But let's say you bump into a stranger at a party and have five minutes to talk. You find her very interesting and engaging. You have lots in common and probably feel like you could keep talking for another hour or so, but there's an unwritten rule that you have to really get to know someone before you call them a friend. Coffee or a beer, another party or event—and more time spent talking—is usually how the dance is done.

The same is true with our donors. They tell you a lot by their behavior. How many times have they given? How much? How recently? All these are clues about the relationship a donor wants with you. However, these don't tell you everything you need to know. A nonprofit assuming a donor should be on a major gifts caseload simply because his gift meets a certain dollar criteria is like following a pleasant stranger around as if he or she wants to be your best friend. Such donors may not want a deeper relationship at all. But for whatever reason, many nonprofits act like that socially awkward guy who thinks anyone who smiles and says hello wants to be his new best buddy.

Here's what we tell nonprofits about how to qualify their donors: First, review what you know about every donor who has met your major gifts criteria in their current giving. That might be $500 or $1,000 cumulative gifts year-to-date. We call this measurement inclination. How is your current donor currently giving, and does he show inclination to give? Next, look at capacity. What is his ability to give? Use any of the wealth indicators to get to this information. When inclination and capacity are both robust, it's time to qualify:

- ✔ **Send an introductory letter.** Explain who you are, thanking the donor for his past support. Let him know you'd like to talk about his interest in your organization and that you'll be calling within the next week.

- ✔ **Make the initial phone call.** Tell the prospect you're following up your letter and that you have been assigned as his personal representative. Thank him for all his past support and say you'd love to know what he is most passionate about regarding your organization. If the donor is forthcoming, try to find out what other organizations he supports, why he likes your organization, and what kind of communication he'd like to have with you in the future. If appropriate, ask if you could sit down to meet with him sometime.

✔ **Mail a survey letter.** If you can't reach the donor by phone after a few tries, leave a message letting her know you called and inviting her to call you back. If you don't hear back within a week, send out another personal letter asking for her feedback in a personal survey. This survey asks questions about the donor's passions, what she values about the organization, what programs she likes the most, and what kind of communications she prefers—basically, all the questions you were going to ask in the phone call. Make sure you include a stamped reply envelope to make it easy for her to respond.

✔ **Send a final note card.** If you still haven't heard from the donor within six weeks, you may want to send one final handwritten note card, asking the donor how he would like to be communicated with. Let him know your contact information.

✔ **Try a final phone call.** Reserve this for those high-dollar donors who have not responded to your previous attempts.

Remember, as we've noted before, you'll probably find that roughly a third of the donors you contact will want a more personal relationship with your organization. Keep in mind you already have a good relationship with some major donors, and you know they will be on your caseload, so you don't need to begin from scratch with donors you already know well. However, sending them a survey, phoning them to thank them, or following up with engaging questions is a good thing.

But here's where many organizations get it wrong. Some MGO caseloads have 450 to 500 donors on them. That's a disaster waiting to happen! The process above can help you take such an unwieldy list and get it down to a size that an MGO can actually manage and serve well.

If you go through this qualification process and discover that your organization has more than 150 qualified major donors for each MGO on your staff, that's a great problem to have—as long as you address it by hiring another MGO so you can give your donors the attention they deserve! It'll be worth your investment.

The process also works effectively for smaller nonprofits where the executive director may be the one who cultivates major donors. We recently helped a small nonprofit take its list of 175 potential major donors down to 45, which is the amount the executive director could handle considering all his other work. This process alone helped raise more than $40,000 in new revenue, because the executive director had time to get in touch with every donor.

Many positives come out of this qualifying process: You learn which donors want to be cultivated in a personal way. You obtain revenue you didn't expect. And you find out what your donors are most passionate about.

You also allow your MGO to scale his efforts to maximize his effectiveness. Think of all the vegetables one person can grow in a small garden. Give that same person a 500-acre farm, and he'd be much less effective. He simply wouldn't know where to start. Reduce the size of your plot, and success will grow.

Decide Which Donors to Contact Most

The subject of caseload composition is a hotly debated topic in major gifts circles, as is the question of how many donors should be on a caseload. As you've already read, we feel that the ideal caseload includes no more than 150 donors. It's possible to work with fewer people, but not more.

As we've also emphasized, these all need to be qualified

donors. This means the MGO has actually spoken to each one personally and is convinced that he or she wants to relate to the organization in a more personal way. In most major gifts programs, people don't bother to find out if the donor wants to personally engage. When an MGO forgets to qualify a caseload of no more than 150 donors, she sets the mechanics of failure into motion.

But even if you have a manageable caseload of 150 qualified donors, you still must decide how to invest your time. What kinds of donors should you be talking with most? This doesn't mean you should worry yourself over gender, age, ethnicity, or political and religious views. Rather, use a selection process that takes two factors into account: each donor's inclination and capacity.

The key measure of a donor's inclination is how recently she has given. If a donor hasn't given in more than a year, she probably should not even be on your caseload! Yet we often get into discussions with MGOs and their managers about why Mr. Smith, who hasn't given for three years, is still a really good prospect. Emotion clouds good judgment, and a trick of perception makes these former donors seem more valuable than the 56 other people who have given sizeable gifts in the last 12 months. It's truly staggering.

A donor's capacity is the measure of how much he is able to give. This is often reflected in his current giving—but not always. Sometimes research will show you that a donor has the potential to give much more.

If you consider both inclination and capacity, with which of the following donors should you spend the most time?

- ▶ A donor who has a net worth of $150 million and made a gift of $100 three years ago.
- ▶ A figure who is very influential in the community, has a lot of connections, and is interested in your cause, but who has never given to your group.
- ▶ A donor who has a net worth of $10 million and gave you $5,000 three months ago.

Let's hope you picked the donor who gave $5,000 recently. Why? Because a lower-net-worth individual who is interested, engaged, and behind you financially—a person who has already demonstrated an inclination to give—is far more important than the person who has huge capacity but little desire to support you. Similarly, someone who can pull strings but never puts her hand in her pocket is not a good candidate for your caseload. The reason these highly influential non-supporters shouldn't be on your caseload is actually very simple: You only have so much time in the day. As far as possible, every minute should be spent developing economic value for your organization. If you use that time to cultivate a relationship with an influential non-donor, be prepared to not reach your economic goals.

Let's say you have your caseload selection criteria nailed down. That leads to the next question: If you're using the criteria of inclination and capacity to select donors for your caseload, and you've qualified them properly, what value should you expect of each donor and how much of your labor should you invest? An effective plan is set forth using the formula below. Assuming you have 150 qualified donors, they should be separated into three tiers:

▶ **A** donors are in your top tier because they have the highest capacity and highest inclination. This group should be the smallest on your caseload, somewhere between 10 percent and 15 percent, but they'll contribute nearly half of the total value.

▶ **B** donors represent the middle group within your caseload. The $5,000 giver in the example above is probably in this group. There are more of them, so they might make up between 40 and 50 percent of your caseload. And they contribute more than a third of the caseload value.

▶ **C** donors are at the lower end of your caseload, contributing the smallest average amounts.

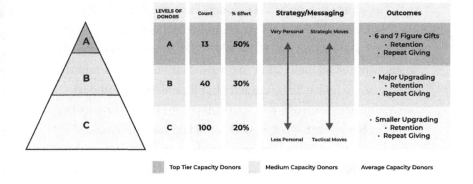

And here are the main things to remember:

▶ You need a top tier of donors who have been identified as having the inclination and capacity to give five-, six-, and even seven-figure gifts. Make it a priority to figure out who these people are and spend a greater portion of your time with them.

▶ You should have two levels of donors below that top tier. Some B donors have capacity to move up into the top tier. Some will move down and join the C donors. Likewise, some of your C donors will move up into the B group. Others will drop out.

▶ Once you've figured out who belongs in which category, manage your time and attention to fit this reality.

It all goes back to the simple concept of the 80/20 rule, which reminds us that most of the results comes from a small percentage of the participants. If you take only one principle from this chapter, let it be that you absolutely must divide your donors into high- to low-value categories.

Proper tiering drives your planning, tells you where to spend your time, and guides your approach to each donor. Without it, you'll wander off course, lose focus, and take action based on emotions and personal preference rather than well thought-out plans and professional duty. And worst of all, you won't achieve your goals.

Make a Plan for Each Donor

Developing a unique plan for every donor on your caseload is no small task. This means there is some "prep" work that needs to be done which includes the following points:

- ✔ **Understand the big picture.** Before creating a plan for each donor, you need to know what the current situation is. This means that for every donor on your caseload you'll need to go through the arduous exercise of evaluating your actions over the past year and analyzing the outcomes. You need to understand what happened in the past to plan effectively for the future.

- ✔ **Incorporate balance.** As you consider your yearly strategic plan for each donor, understand the delicate balance in the type and timing of your communications. Over the course of the year, aim for an ongoing cycle of communications that include asking, thanking, and sending YMAD (You Made a Difference) touches, along with personal notes.

- ✔ **Cash-flow your revenue goals.** This is simply making an educated guess about when to expect revenue from each donor. We've talked about creating the goals earlier. Now you need to give your best estimate for when those gifts will come in. For example, your goal for one of your donors might be $50,000—$25,000 in March and $25,000 in December. Trust us, you want this. Here's why:

    - It keeps you focused.
    - It helps you design your plan.
    - It allows you and senior management to consider when to expect revenue.
    - It holds you accountable with a monthly revenue goal.

- ✔ **Start building your plan.** Now that you have a revenue goal for each donor and you have it cash-flowed by month, you're ready to create a strategic plan. To put it simply, the strategic plan is the answer for how you're going to make your goals. Remember, following the communication cycle is key here. And knowing what's happening with your organization during the course of the year is critical. What events is your organization sponsoring? What volunteer opportunities are there? What kinds of mailings are being sent by the direct-response program? These are all important things you might use in your plan. Don't just make a spontaneous decision to ask for a gift. Know when you're going to do it, why you're going to do it, and exactly what leads up to it.

✔ Know your donor. Really understanding each donor— her passions, the type of person she is, and how she likes to be communicated with. This knowledge should drive your strategy. If you know your donor is interested in helping children in Haiti, you're not going to send her an article on elder care in Honduras. Each donor wants to feel known, not treated exactly like everyone else. Keep this in mind as you plan.

✔ Ensure a good mix. Part of incorporating balance in communications involves making sure the contact is varied, and not just a string of asks or thank-you notes. Combine asks with appropriate personal touches, like birthday and holiday cards. Remember to spread YMAD touches throughout the year and include the occasional mass organizational piece. Some touches are highly personal; others communicate more broadly—but a good rule of thumb is to schedule one or more a month.

✔ Write the actual plan on a calendar. You may have sophisticated software that allows you to connect your plan to your calendar. But you don't need software to get this work done. Quite simply, you can just make a spreadsheet with all of your donors running down the left side and the months spread horizontally across the top. This plan will serve as a constant reminder of your goals for each day. Creating a strategic plan for each of your donors is essential to keeping you focused, disciplined and accountable. But most important, it will go a long way toward helping you reach your goals.

Remember: Every Donor is Different

It's really hard to believe that a seasoned major gifts professional would, in a moment of temporary insanity, tell his team to "just mail the caseload an ask!"

Yet it happens all the time.

What got into this good professional's mind? How did he get off track? What caused him to depart from what he knows works best and, instead, to mail a direct-marketing appeal to the organization's highest-level donors?

Major gifts officers and major gift managers sometimes lose their way on this point because:

- ▶ They really haven't been managing the donors on their caseloads as individuals, so they find it easy and expedient to just mail an identical appeal to all of them.

- ▶ They have forgotten that relationship building takes time and, in an act of impatience, they treat all major donors as if they were the same.

- ▶ They don't really know what to do with their donors. Lacking a plan for each donor, they revert to a direct-marketing strategy that they know won't work but hold out hope that it does.

- ▶ They've forgotten that every donor is different. Each qualified major donor requires individual, customized attention.

Whatever the reason, this business of approaching every donor in the same way is major gifts suicide. It can kill your program! You can't possibly experience real success in major gifts until you give your effort over to the idea that each donor is a unique individual with special, singular characteristics, motivations, and interests.

If you intimately know each of the donors on your caseload, you should be able to place them into a value hierarchy from 1 to 150, devoting proportionately more time, energy, and thought with the donors at the top of the list and progressively less nearing the bottom. It's a fact: Not all donors are the same. Because they differ in potential and value, you must have a value hierarchy for your caseload.

But here's the problem. Unless you've worked with your entire caseload for several years and know each donor intimately, you can't easily and accurately place each individual in a hierarchy of value. No one can get to know people that quickly and find all their hunches are correct.

Which is why, until you accumulate at least two years' worth of knowledge and experience, you must do the next best thing: Classify your donors, or tier them, into the three groups mentioned earlier in the chapter. Whatever point in the year you're reading this, it's not too late to start. Even if it's already the fourth quarter, work on this now so you can benefit from it next year.

Focus Your Efforts

Lately, we have encountered two situations in which MGOs have refused to do the kind of planning and prioritizing that we have suggested. These MGOs have let impulsive behavior drive what they do with their caseload donors on any given day. And guess what? Both have encountered financial disasters that have jeopardized their careers. Each is running the risk of losing his job, for no reason other than sheer stubbornness.

In one case, the MGO had originally carefully followed the simple advice we've laid out and had found great success at cultivating two donors who each gave six-figure gifts in a previous financial year! This year, however, he chose just to follow his impulses, and the numbers have been quite bad. When we asked him what he thought the reason for the poor performance was, he said, "Well, I didn't prioritize my caseload like I did last year." And why didn't he? He had no explanation.

The other MGO—against all evidence and experience to the contrary—continues to function as if all the donors on her caseload are the same. So she spends her time coming up with a communication plan for her entire caseload, not for each individual donor. The numbers are sliding, and things are getting dicey, yet she refuses to acknowledge that she's headed down a disastrous path. We guess it will take a bad review or being put on probation to get her attention. It's a sad situation, partly because it's so unnecessary.

We have spent more than twenty years navigating the ups and downs of major giving. We know that this kind of focused approach works—it has been proven many times over. So why do some MGOs find this strategy for a major gifts program so difficult to actually own and operate? Sheer laziness alone can't be the answer; people often work just as hard at doing the wrong things as they do at doing the right things.

To succeed in this major gifts work, you must prioritize or tier your donors. You need to devote your primary attention to a small group of **A** donors who are your highest-value donors in terms of both current giving and capacity. Don't put people in this category based only on their capacity to give. If donors have a high capacity but aren't giving substantially now, don't rate them with an **A**.

Again, we believe you should have no more than 10 or 15 **A** donors in your caseload of 150. There could be a couple more, but don't load this category up. Why? Because you're going to spend 50 percent of your time on the donors in this category! Half of your time. They have the highest potential, so they will invariably respond to your highest investment of time. Your plans and moves with these donors will be very personal and very strategic, with clear plans designed to retain them as donors, to secure additional gifts, and to upgrade to larger gifts.

Your **B** donors and **C** donors should progressively require less time. With them, your strategy and messaging is more tactical and less personal. Not as intense.

In terms of outcomes and objectives for each donor group, retention and repeat giving is a key outcome that you want for every donor. The primary difference between the **B** and **C** donors is major upgrading for the **B** donors and smaller upgrading for the **C** donors.

The benefit of using this approach is the ability to stratify the caseload so you know where to spend your time. You will find that if you do this, you'll have success over the long haul.

Pause for Thought:
The Worst Day of My Career
Jeff Schreifels

When I began my second job in development, I was in my late twenties and eager to make my mark in the world. I'd been hired as the development director of a small nonprofit that trained people with disabilities in computer technology. We would start with people who were on public assistance or disability payments and we'd eventually see them find high-paying jobs in the computer industry. What a great mission!

It was a small shop, so I had to do a little bit of everything: annual fund appeals, events, grant-writing, and cultivating major gifts. The diversity proved to be great fun.

About a month into the job, I had reviewed files on all our major donors. I came up with a list of people who hadn't given in a couple of years or more. One of those donors was a board member, and I was salivating. Here was a dedicated board member who hadn't given in two years—and I knew this guy had money. I could see that a huge gift was ripe for the picking.

I talked with the president of the nonprofit and told him I wanted to meet with this board member and get to know him. The president was more than happy to have me do this. So, I set up the meeting and drove out to the board member's workplace.

Even though I'd told this board member that I just wanted to meet and get to know him, all I could think about on my drive there was how I was going to ask him for $20,000 and come back with a check to present to my boss. And I knew that when

I got back to the office with that check, the president would shake my hand, pop the champagne, and wonder why he hadn't hired me years ago. What a joyous day it was going to be!

There was just one problem. When I finally got to his office and sat down with the board member, all he wanted to talk about was his work, his wife and kids, and his recent vacation. I was sort of rolling my eyes and paying very little attention. All I was looking for was the right opportunity to ask him for the money.

Finally, there was a pause in the conversation. Time to strike. "So," I said, "you've been a board member for about four years, and I noticed you haven't given in the last 24 months. I'm wondering if you could make a $20,000 gift today?"

Victory! I had said it. I made the big ask.

He was a little surprised at first, and seemed quite flustered. "What?" he said. "Um . . . I don't . . . wait, hmm . . . yeah, I think I can do that. I might need to move some things around, but I . . . I think that's doable."

Joy! I shook his hand, quickly said goodbye, and swept out patting myself on the back. I rushed back to the office to tell the president the great news. "I am truly awesome," I thought. "Here I am, only one month into the job, and I've already landed the biggest individual contribution in this nonprofit's history!"

When I arrived, the president was already at the door waiting to greet me. But he didn't have a smile on his face. He said, "Jeff, could you come into my office?" It didn't sound like good news. The door clicked shut.

"What on earth happened with Tom? He just called and said you had blindsided him by asking for a $20,000 gift. He was so taken aback by this brashness that he felt obligated to say yes. But he's decided he will not make such a gift. And he just resigned from the board!"

The knot in my stomach was agonizing. I thought I would keel over and die on the spot. Fortunately for me, my boss was a man of great compassion and grace. He knew my intentions were good, but my methods were . . . well, let's just say it didn't come off as I'd intended. I learned a lot that day, definitely the worst day of my professional career. And things eventually got better. Some time later, I was able to go back to Tom and apologize. Soon afterward he came back to the board of directors—and eventually he did give us that $20,000.

It was an undeserved happy ending, one that came about despite my having ignored just about every principle of donor relations described in this book. Here's a recap of what went wrong:

- ▶ I went after the money, not the relationship. I was thinking only about bringing back that check instead of developing a friendship with the donor.
- ▶ I didn't do my research. Had I done more investigating, I would have known that Tom had started a new business two years earlier and was struggling financially.
- ▶ I didn't listen. Tom was trying to tell me who he was and what he cared about, but all I could think about was how to make the big ask.
- ▶ I had no plan. I hadn't thought about where I wanted to go with Tom or any other major donor. I just was going to charge in and make them cough up some money.
- ▶ I didn't look at the donor as a partner in mission. I looked at him as a source of cash. Even worse, I saw him as someone who owed the organization a donation, because he was on the board, hadn't given in a while, and was supposedly loaded. Gosh, how arrogant could I have been?

Yes, it was the worst day of my career, but I also grew up that day. While I still remember it as an incredibly painful experience, it allowed me to reflect and change the way I approached major gifts fundraising.

I also learned a lot about grace, forgiveness, and second chances. I always have appreciated the way my boss handled that situation. He allowed me to make a huge mistake and learn from it. Others might have walked off and fired me.

Chapter 9
Creating Effective Donor Offers

"I don't have anything to present to donors," the MGO said. And his manager, a little impatient, said: "Just look around you. Look at all the things we are doing. Get out there and get familiar with them, and then you will know what to present to donors!"

That sums up the dilemma almost every MGO faces as they try to do their best to raise funds for the organization they serve. It is one of the most misunderstood areas in major gift fundraising, one that raises the hackles of many managers who expect their MGOs to go out into the marketplace and "get the money."

We were in one meeting where we were talking about the need for more resources for the MGOs to present to donors, and the manager went off for over 15 minutes. She "did not understand what the problem is here. For goodness sakes, everyone sitting around this table knows what we do! This is not rocket science. What's the problem?"

So, we patiently explained that one of the major reasons her team of very gifted and competent MGOs had not secured larger gifts was because they had nothing to present to donors. That what they did have was general program descriptions and a finance department that was not helpful in giving information and that, given these circumstances, it was impossible to be effective.

The manager was visibly irritated and impatient. But we continued.

Richard said: "Look at it this way. If this were a manufacturing plant, would you expect all the employees to bring their own tools and the raw materials to produce the product? Or if this was a retail store, would you expect all the employees to find and bring in the product they were going to sell and locate shelves, store signage and cash registers in order to process the sales? No, you would provide the product and tools necessary to help the employee do their job. But there is hardly any other example in any organization that we know of, commercial or not, where the employee is not only required to be good at selling and dealing with customers, but they also have to come up with the product to sell."

The manager was still irritated. But we had made the point. They needed to work together with program, finance and frontline people to come up with "products" to present to donors. And if we helped them to do that well, we would see more major donors upgraded and more six- and seven-figure gifts come in.

The Old Way of Doing Things Is Changing

Here's what most non-profits do with their numbers and financial information. The focus of their number crunching is on maintaining old accounting categories and practices, rather than presenting life-saving programs to their donors. This old and antiquated system is hurting fundraisers which, in turn, is hurting the organization as it becomes increasingly difficult to raise money.

There is nothing wrong with the idea that nonprofits should follow standardized accounting procedures *internally*. But many good financial managers who use this system don't realize that without a change in the way they use these reports with MGOs and donors, they are damaging efforts to raise the support that they're accounting for.

When major gift officers work from standard budget lines to discover how much it will cost for a donor to support a program or project, they end up missing significant costs (overhead) that are vital and necessary for the program to continue. Then because this overhead is not being raised, MGOs face pressure from management to "get the money" in unrestricted gifts—which we know is far from easy.

Add to this struggle the fact that the donors are changing, too.

Joshua Birkholz, in his book *Fundraising Analytics*, says, "Donors are approaching philanthropy in a completely different way. They are making decisions more thoughtfully. Their gifts are following their own intended purposes. Donors are seeking a return on their philanthropic investments. And they desire an increased level of personalization. Organizations embracing this change are climbing a mountain of success, while others, forcing their own models onto their donors, are fighting in the foothills."

We must never forget that donors choose to give because they want to make the world a better place. After donating to causes they are passionate about, they like to learn the measurable effect of their gifts. A bottom-line figure in an outdated annual report, some accounting mumbo jumbo, a glossy marketing brochure or some program description that is too general doesn't get the job done anymore. Nor does it tell the donor what he or she wants or needs to know.

It is a fact that donors are changing. They are expecting more in their relationships with their favorite charities. And that is why it is so important for a non-profit to "package their program and budget," a process we at Veritus Group call the Donor Impact Portfolio (DIP for short). There are three important reasons why an organization should implement a program and budget packaging process:

1. To directly address the changing donor landscape and their requirements.
2. To support the fundraising, marketing and communication functions of the organization by providing specific program information and pricing so that fundraisers can more effectively raise money.
3. To reduce donor value attrition, which averages 40-60% in most organizations and represents **multiple millions of dollars lost every year.**

The Donor Impact Portfolio will show donors specifically what their money will "buy." It also addresses the five most common problems that currently exist within most non-profits related to finances and the budget:

1. The budget is organized for organizational purposes, not for donors.
2. The program part of the budget is understated, and therefore fundraisers are not focused on raising the total amount needed.
3. Overhead is seen as a necessary evil, not as an integral part of program.
4. It is almost impossible for fundraisers to represent what the organization does and quantify it because (a) they cannot get to the numbers within a program category and (b) the budget cannot be presented in ways the donor thinks and supports, i.e., in terms of what is being done for people and/or the planet.
5. Because of this situation, fundraisers and donors will tend to want to fund programs that are outside the budget, causing even more problems internally.

All of this results in a financial situation that younger, more inquisitive and business-minded donors find troubling and sloppy; the organization runs the risk of losing support from this very important and growing constituency.

Gone are the days when a donor just gives to your cause because "I trust them." There may be trust, but they will want to verify how things operate and more importantly, they will be thinking about what the organization accomplishes in specific categories and impact, not in accounting terms. That is why we created this approach to packaging the program and budget.

Principles of Packaging the Program and Budget into a Donor Impact Portfolio

The idea of program and budget packaging is based on these principles:

- ▶ **Current Program Budget**: You'll be packaging the program and budget of what the organization *currently does* for people and the planet in an integrated manner. And this view goes down to the smallest level of the organization so that donors can grasp and support what is happening in every part of the organization. The reason we focus on current program is because that is what the current budget is all about. Our job in major gifts is first to secure funds for the current program—not something new.

- ▶ **All Costs Are In**: It means that ALL the costs are included, both direct and overhead. Most fundraisers are only securing the direct program costs with their fundraising, NOT the overhead. This is a huge problem and one of the reasons many non-profits are in financial trouble.

- ▶ **The End Result**: This process creates packages that cover a broad selection of things a donor can support in the current program. It could be children, youth, young adults, couples, seniors, animals, the environment, issues of justice, the arts, economic development, education, health care, drug rehab, single parent care, child care, job training, spiritual work, housing, feeding, etc.—any number of ways to help. And the donors could look at it as all of the above PLUS a specific PLACE that they are interested in.

It also means that there are different "price points" to any and all categories of help. So, if the donor wants a $1,000 project, she can find it. Or if it is $10,000 or $3 million, she can also find it. When you package your program and budget you will want to have a "portfolio" of current program opportunities a donor can fund. Portfolio is defined as "a group of possible investments donors can have in an area they are interested in."

Donors Won't Pay for Overhead!

You may have noticed that we are advocating that you include overhead expenses in your packaged programs. That's right—and we believe it's essential. But there is something about overhead that is so toxic to major gift officers that they literally run away from it every time it gets close to them.

And it's not only MGOs that are repulsed by the topic. Managers and leaders feel pretty squeamish about it too. You bring up the subject and you can see their bodies tighten, as they get ready to defend this nasty but necessary thing.

We were in a meeting once with some managers where the "O" word came up. You would think we had just moved into the ring of a major boxing match. Goodness. Some managers were defensive. Others quietly retreated into their spreadsheets. Still others moved into some language about "We're doing the best we can to keep costs down."

So, we stepped into this swamp with the following question: "What do you think donors think about overhead?" And we were off on a fun journey that mixed one cup of philosophy with another cup of reality and ten pounds of anxiety.

The core assumption in this meeting, and in non-profits in general, is that major donors do not like, nor will they pay for, overhead. This is wrong for several reasons.

Overhead is a good thing. What?! A good thing? Yep. And we need to start talking it up. No more of this sniveling, shifty, wandering into a dark corner about this subject. We need to embrace it for the good that it is.

Overhead is necessary. Here is what is so funny about this topic. If you didn't have overhead you wouldn't have anything. It is still mind blowing to us to sit in a meeting with seemingly intelligent people and have them imply that overhead is bad, must be pushed down to levels that make it impossible to run the organization and must be hidden in financial reports so ill-informed donors can't find or discern where they are or how much they are. This is truly comical.

There was another meeting where Richard got into quite a heated debate with a top finance guy on the need for overhead. You should have heard the positions he was taking. It was like we were on a different planet. Richard would say, "But, Bill (not his real name), you just cannot run this organization on the 10% you are saying you run it on. Your costs are really in the 20-26% range. Why don't you just come out with it?" "Because the donors won't pay for it, Richard. That's why!" And they went round and round.

Here's a guy, not unlike hundreds we have met, who (a) really believes overhead is nasty, (b) can't find a way to tell the truth about it, and (c) is trapped in the circular argument he has created. Richard even made the following argument: "OK, Bill, let's eliminate this overhead item and that overhead item, etc. Now, can you run the program?" He had to admit he couldn't, which made Richard's point. Overhead is a necessary and needed part of pulling off the mission of the organization. Why is it that we can't get this in our heads?!?

The non-profit world and the watchdogs have perpetuated a misconception about overhead. There are many people out there, non-profit leaders and self-appointed watchdogs, who find virtue in propagating the idea that overhead under 20% is right up there with sainthood. Unbelievable. And for many of these people, when you look under the blankets in their organizations, the real number is far higher than what they are publishing—they simply have adopted sophisticated legal ways of packaging it all. We wouldn't say it's ethical—but it is legal. This just causes more pressure on the sector and keeps donors in the dark on the subject. There are a few glimmers of light out there on this subject with some leaders who are showing courage by speaking out and taking action. But it is slow in coming.

Do This First

So now that we've laid out the rationale for setting up to package the program and budget of your organization, before even beginning to implement it, let's consider some steps you need to take first, to ensure the success of this exercise:

1. **First, get YOUR head right about this issue.** The way we've worked through this topic to get to a balanced place was to look at how much effort it takes to make a product or make a profit in a commercial company. We also looked at how much effort it takes to get anything done. What we mean is that when you start to examine the relationship of the effort put out to achieve a result, you begin to understand that it takes far more effort to get a result. When you really look at this in a number of areas of life, you'll see that the relationship of cause and effect—of effort to make something happen vs. achieving the result—was a lot larger than you may think. If all you had to do in life was make a 10% effort and get a huge result, life would be easy. You might have had a different path, but stop and think about this a bit. And ask yourself the question—what DOES it take to get the program delivered in a non-profit? And how important a role does overhead play in making program happen? Your honest answer will help you land in a better place.

2. **Realize that major donors can understand how overhead is a critical part of delivering program.** More and more, enlightened donors are really getting it in this area. They know what it takes to get things done. Many major donors are businesspeople and entrepreneurs. They know what they went through to be successful. They know what overhead they had

to have to make things work. They really do understand. But YOU need to talk sensibly about this. And that is why…

3. **You can make a difference in this area.** If you start talking about overhead in a calm, professional and sensible way, you can start to change this around as your donors begin to understand that delivering life-changing help to people and to our planet will not happen without these basic support systems in place.

4. **Make sure your leadership is on board with Program and Budget Packaging.** Believe it or not, we have seen multiple situations in large and small non-profits where the fund-raising "troops" are yearning for more program information to present to donors, but upper management (including the top leader) is totally indifferent to the idea. The top person actually does not know where the money comes from! Unbelievable. Getting top leaders on board is vital. We have been involved in situations where the top people wag their heads in agreement to this approach, but do not mandate it down through finance and program. At other times, a relatively low-level finance person was holding the entire organization hostage by not implementing the program because "he just didn't think it was worth the effort." A good leader will make the difference in seeing the process through.

5. **Make sure program understands what you are trying to do.** You may find this hard to believe, but many program people do not know where the money comes from in their organization. Can you say "DONORS"??? This is another unbelievable dynamic in many non-profits. The program people are so focused on "doing" program that they cannot give any time or attention to service the donors, the very source of their funding! Now, there are a lot of program people who have this right. But we've been around this long enough to know you had better make sure the program folks are with you on this, before you dive into implementing Program and Budget Packaging.

6. **Make sure there is a commitment to allocating overhead to program categories.** OK, as we have said earlier in this chapter, this is a BIG one—a really big one. We have attended meetings with intelligent, competent, well placed professionals in some pretty impressive organizations, and they told us they could not support allocating organizational overhead to individual program categories and projects. So, in a $50 million dollar organization you could have $10-12 million in overhead that just sits there and can't be raised without going through all kinds of rather dubious tricks and sleight of hand moves to make the ratios turn out fine. This is another unbelievable situation. In one case, a leader of a large non-profit was asked, "So, do you think, Al (not his real name), that you could run this organization without that $10 million in overhead?" "Of course not," he said, "don't be silly. Of course we couldn't do it." So, we followed up with, "Well then, what you are saying is that you need this overhead to deliver the program, right? And it then seems that proportionately allocating the organizational overhead to each of the programs and projects makes sense. It's an actual cost of doing the program!" He would not hear of it. Although we felt like screaming, we took a breath and moved on. You need to gain a commitment from the "powers that be" on allocating your overhead to program categories.

The Process

So, once you set the stage and get your organization on board, how do you package your programs and budget?

First, with leadership, program and fundraising folks at the table, **come up with a definitive list of program categories and sub-categories.** You might think you already have these because they are on your website and annual report. Believe us, this doesn't mean anything. We have seen websites and annual reports that label program with marketing labels, not program. We have seen websites and annual reports that list accounting categories instead of program categories and sub-categories. We have seen annual reports and websites that list program categories that are obviously not thought out and don't make much sense. Now is a good time to get everyone in a room and ask the questions, "What do we do? What are the categories and sub-categories? How can we say it in a donor-centered way? What are the sub-categories?" etc.

Next, **create definitions (descriptions) for each program category**. This is important so that everyone is on the same page about what the category means.

Divide the entire budget into your list of program categories and sub-categories, including any program expenses that may be sitting in departments/divisions that mostly are overhead cost centers. As you are dividing the budget down, pay special attention to types of people served or types of beneficiaries (i.e., for an animal charity it might be grouping costs by types of animals) and location or geography (i.e., where the money is being spent). Why? Because donors are interested in the program category AND the type of people served AND where it all happens: category, beneficiary and location. So, as you are dividing the budget down, make sure you have a matrix that captures this information for each program category.

Allocate any remaining overhead proportionately to the program categories. The result of implementing this point will be that, whereas you started with an organizational budget of $50 million which divided down into $12 million of overhead and $38 million of direct program expense, you now have a list of program categories, each one sub-divided into program beneficiaries and location—the whole list totaling $50 million dollars —an actual "shopping list" of programs and projects ready for presentation to donors.

Remember, this exercise is NOT about organizational ratios for watchdog agencies. That reporting thing still needs to happen as it does now. This has nothing to do with that. This is exclusively about packaging your entire budget into program categories for presentation to donors to secure their support. Conceptually, if all your donors "bought" every single one of your categories, your entire budget would be raised, including the overhead. That is the objective.

We think you can see that, performed correctly, this new source of information will revolutionize fundraising. MGOs and your other fundraising staff, for the first time, will have an organizational budget that actually translates into a list of programs and projects that donors can support.

Program and Budget Packaging will make an MGO's life better. If you've actually gone through the whole exercise of packaging your program and budget for donors, you will have each and every fundraiser in your organization literally kissing your feet in appreciation. Why? Because you have made their jobs so much easier. Remember, the MGO's job is to maintain and build a relationship with a donor. It is not his or her job to come up with the "product." Yet, even as we write this, there are thousands of MGOs out there struggling to come up with something to show their donors, while the managers and leaders of these good folks turn their backs on them, at the same time expecting them to perform. This is not right. But now you know what to do.

How You Can Use Packaged Programs and Budgets

How can you use the information you've created through this process? Obviously, you can pull out information for major donor asks, based on their passions and interests, and include that MUCH more easily in your presentations.

But this is far from the end of the usefulness of packaged programs and budgets. Here are other some ideas, not listed in any particular order of importance:

1. *Reports of all types.* Use the packaged information to tell donors and other publics what you are doing and how much you are spending in each program category. This system is a good source for annual reports.

2. *Direct mail.* Packaged program and budget information can be used to formulate offers and asks for direct mail appeals, newsletters and receipt letters and stuffers. In newsletters, this information can be very helpful to more fully explain what you are doing in a specific category.
3. *Online content.*
4. *Brochures and collateral.* Use packaged program and budget information to create category brochures or other collateral which explains the various program initiatives of the organization.
5. *Radio, television and other electronic media.* Packaged program and budget information can be used to explain how funds are used, or for offer/ask creation in documentaries and fundraising efforts for radio, television, the production of DVDs, CDs and other forms of electronic media.
6. *Events.* Use packaged program and budget information to frame offers, asks and project presentations for events.
7. *Major donor programs.* As mentioned above, packaged program and budget information can be used to match the donor's passions and interests to a category of program service and thereby create an offer or ask that is appropriate for the donor.
8. *Planned Giving.* When explaining to a donor how her planned giving involvement with the organization can help, the packaged program and budget information can be a critical piece for making your case as to how the donor's funds can be used.
9. *Capital Campaigns.* While capital campaigns are usually forward-looking, i.e., building something in the future to meet a current need, the packaged program and budget information can be useful in explaining how similar programs to the one being planned for in the capital campaign have worked in the past and how this one will work in the future.

10. Foundation Proposals. Use packaged program and budget information to create foundation proposals that match the funding criteria of the foundation.

11. Church and club presentations. Packaged program and budget information can be used to create projects for churches and social clubs, matching their areas of interest to the categories in your program packages and budgets.

These are just a few ways you can use the packaged budget and program information not only to raise money but also to report back to donors on how money is being used. You can marry the packaged financial information to results statistics in the creation of powerful feedback to donors on how their money was used and what a difference it made.

One thing is for sure: if you can pull this off (admittedly, this will not be easy), you will see tremendous growth in your revenue as it becomes easier and easier to tell your donor WHY you need the money and WHAT you did with it.

With these two critical and strategic arenas as the key drivers for successful fundraising, we at Veritus can't imagine why any MGO would want to do his or her job without this information.

Chapter 10:
Permission-Based Asking

Asking for a gift is the cornerstone of fundraising. If you haven't asked for a gift, you are not a fundraiser. Every successful nonprofit must have robust systems and structures that create opportunities for donors to contribute to fulfilling the mission.

Despite the fact that asking is, in our opinion, THE key to fundraising overall, and specifically to a major gifts program, many organizations fail at it.

You can fail at asking just as easily as you can be successful with it.

If your organization is going after a donor's money, you are failing. If you do not have a fundraising culture centered on knowing, appreciating, and honoring a donor's passions and interests, you are doing it wrong. If you do not have meaningful opportunities for a donor to give a transformational gift, you are missing the boat.

Asking the right way is the difference between your organization surviving the many challenges facing nonprofits, or not. You have to take this seriously.

In this chapter, we are going to be talking about four key

topics that will deepen your connection to your donors, create a culture of philanthropy in your organization, and help you create the right ask.

1. The first part introduces you to the Veritus Group Permission-Based Asking Model™ where we lay the basis for a new and effective philosophy and system for asking.
2. Then we deal with how to **prepare** to use the asking model.
3. Next, we cover how to integrate what you have prepared into the asking model.
4. And lastly, how to deal with your donor's responses, questions and concerns.

The Permission-Based Asking Model™

Most asking strategies are about getting the money—some of them even approach manipulation. And that is wrong. What is needed is an asking model or system that honors the donor in the giving process while asking effectively. That is why we created the Veritus Group Permission-Based Asking Model™.

This model is a major change in how donors are asked to become involved with the causes they love and support.

The model blends the most current concepts of thought leaders in the commercial marketplace on how to honor and retain customers, with the best practices from the non-profit world on donor and value retention.

Here is some background.

In 1999, Seth Godin observed that successful campaigns were the ones that sought the customer's consent. From that core idea he wrote the book *Permission Marketing: Turning Strangers into Friends and Friends into Customers,* published on May 6, 1999.

Permission marketing allows consumers to choose whether or not to be subjected to marketing. This choice results in better engagement and customer retention.

The Permission-Based Asking Model™ is based on the concept that a fundraiser should ask for permission to become a partner in fulfilling the donor's passions and interests. Interesting concept, isn't it? Asking permission to ask. We don't usually think about asking in this way—we just ask, presuming it's OK. This is why donors feel abused—why they feel like cash dispensers—why they don't feel valued and honored.

Here's what it looks like:

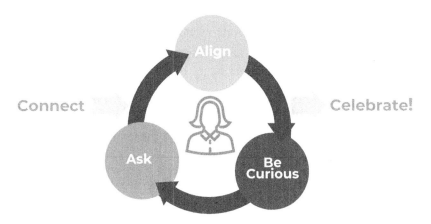

Copyright © 2019 Veritus Group LLC

There are three important concepts to keep in mind when using this model:

1. At every step, you must always ask permission. This is about honoring and respecting the donor and, in your heart and mind, holding her in high esteem and treating her as an equal. This is not about the donor's money. It's about helping the donor fulfill her passions and interests.

2. The model starts with connection, then moves into a circular process of alignment, curiosity and asking. The reason this part is circular is because alignment needs to occur at every point of the donor interaction. Often an ask does not result in a clear path. For instance, you might ask and get "let me think about it" in return. This forces a replay of the alignment process where you:

- Confirm that the donor wants to "think about it."
- Ask questions (be curious) about why, so you understand.
- Ask if it would be OK to contact the donor later.

There's always a need to let the alignment process function for any type of answer or situation you may encounter.

3. The model or process ends with celebration, no matter what occurred in the alignment process. If, at the end of alignment, the answer is:

- **Yes**— then you celebrate what will happen in people's lives or on the planet because of the donor's gift. You fill the donor's heart with the joy of knowing what she has just accomplished.
- **Maybe**— then you celebrate what COULD happen. You celebrate the partnership with the donor and their interest in changing the world.
- **No**— then you celebrate what has been accomplished by the past giving of the donor and their continued passion and interest to change X.

This celebration point is missed in most asking strategies and models. That's because those strategies focus on getting the money rather than celebrating what the donor has accomplished. Don't make that mistake. Your main objective in fundraising is to fulfill the donor's passions and interests, not to secure the money. The money is a result of fulfilling the donor's passions and interests.

There are two important roles you'll need to play as you use this model with a donor:

1. The Partner Role: The partner role is where you're working through the model with the objective of fulfilling the donor's passions and interests. In every phase of the model your heart, spirit and behavior is tuned in to serving the donor through your connection and alignment to her, asking questions and clarifying, asking for the gift, and finally celebrating what's been accomplished. You must keep this focus as you're going through each phase of the model.

2. *The Facilitator Role:* Having a good facilitator at any meeting is extremely helpful. In this role you are facilitating a natural and engaging conversation using great open-ended questions and managing the transitions from one phase of the conversation to the next. You are fully present to your donor, actively listening, and ensuring you are a true partner in this process. In doing this, your donor feels heard and understood and you're respecting the donor's time and ensuring that the phases are covered in your meeting. The speed and rhythm of this will change depending on the time you have and the personality of the donor.

Oh, there is one more very fascinating and useful feature of this model. It can be used to ask for anything in any situation. Just think of any aspect of your life—personal or professional—where you need to ask for something. Now go through the steps of connection, alignment, curiosity, asking and celebration. You'll find that this works in every situation where you need to ask someone else for something. You'll see how this works in a practical way as we get further into the details.

And remember, as you're dealing with your caseload donors, keep honoring them by being curious about their passions and interests. Keep serving those passions and interests with passion, energy, and care—and make sure you're asking permission along the way.

Making Connections

Before you move into this phase, we want to be sure that you have the following things in place:

1. Do you have a current relationship? Is the donor *qualified*, or are you just approaching them cold? By "qualified" we mean you've already been in contact with them and they have signaled that they want to relate to you one-on-one. If you haven't done this, don't proceed with this model. It won't work. You must have a current relationship.

2. **Do you know the passions and interests of the donor?** If not, you must secure that information first. It's not enough to know the donor or have talked with him or her. You must have a clear grasp of what drives the donor's giving motivations so you can properly engage and have an authentic, integrated and clear conversation with the donor. (We've written a lot about this, and you can find more information on the Passionate Giving website (https://veritusgroup.com/passionate-giving-blog/)—just search for "passions and interests.")

OK, let's say you're good with the two items above. Now you need to secure a meeting. We have written extensively about this as well. And it's not an easy task. But remember this: the ONLY reason a donor will not meet with you is because you don't have anything of value to share.

So, the secret to getting the meeting is to give the donor something of value. And that value lies in serving their passions and interests—giving them a steady diet of information that they are interested in so that they *want* to meet with you. You can read about getting meetings on our website (https://veritusgroup.com/intro-to-five-relationship-steps-in-getting-meetings/) before you go on.

OK, you've secured a meeting, and now you're face-to-face with the donor. It's time to connect. That's the sole objective of this phase—to emotionally connect with the donor and to get into the present moment together.

Perhaps you talk about a trip the donor just took, or the child the donor just dropped off at college, or the surgery the donor had, or the life circumstance she has been telling you about. It needs to be something that matters to the donor and signals that you are now here and present.

You begin by saying something like: "Before we begin our meeting, I'd love to hear more about…"—and then you authentically process the information the donor gives.

You've arrived at a natural transition point. You'll know it because the donor is obviously done answering your question. When you get to this point, then you move to your facilitator role and you ask for permission to move on—you signal transition to *alignment*.

Doing this confirms that you are the facilitator of this meeting, ensuring that things move forward as needed. And it gets you to the next phase of the asking model.

That's the essence of the "connect phase" of the model. Stated simply: you are connecting with the donor in a manner that shows the donor you know her and are present to her and her passions and interests.

This isn't an easy task, so don't let yourself think that connecting in this way is no big deal. It isn't. But if you are thoughtful about it, and you let the donor's passions and interests (plus the personal knowledge you have acquired about her) drive the interaction you will, indeed, connect emotionally—and you'll be on your way toward the next step of the asking model.

The Alignment Circle

One of the biggest errors in asking is to assume that the process is linear, i.e., you start at one point and, through a succession of steps, you get to the final conclusion. As if the steps are all in order, like stakes in the ground—where you complete one step, then move to another, then another and then you're done.

We don't think this is how real life and relationships work. Nor is it effective.

You know as well as we do that real-life interaction with others is circular. You start the interaction in one place and then receive a reaction. If you are operating with a belief that honoring the other person is important (as we do), then you take that reaction and adjust—rather than just plowing through with your agenda. This is delicate.

And this is why we call this part of Permission-Based Asking™ the *Alignment Circle*—because it's that part of the "system" where you seek to align to the donor and her passions and interests.

Please note several things about the alignment circle:

First, you always need to keep the donor in the center of the alignment. That is why we put a symbolic figure at the center—this is to help you remember that the donor must be at the center, and she must be the decision-maker.

Then there are three integrated steps in the circle as follows:

1. **Align**— The sole objective of this phase is agreement, understanding and alignment about whatever topic comes up, either as you enter the alignment circle or as you go all the way around and a new topic or issue surfaces. This is where you seek to understand; and as you understand, you agree and align. So, as you enter the alignment circle, your first level of alignment might be as simple as confirming the reason for your call or visit and the time that is available. It sounds like this: "As we discussed over the phone, I'm here to talk with you about an opportunity for you to have a great impact on xxx; is that your understanding? And does meeting until XX time still work for you today?"

There is another important value that you should pay attention to in this alignment step. It is to consistently and constantly empower the donor, encouraging them to be themselves in the interaction with you and not responding in an obligatory manner to your presence or your words.

Once I (Richard) was with a CEO of a major non-profit in the Midwest. She was telling me that she gets so many calls from charities seeking her support. I asked if she gave to them. "Yes," she replied, "I feel obligated." So, here is a situation where the donor does not feel empowered—empowered to say what she really thinks, empowered to say no, empowered to ask the question that she wants to ask, etc.

This empowering item is so important. You are confirming

and empowering the donor to express her passions and interests through the work of your organization. You are ensuring that she understands that her partnership with you is something that means a lot to you.

Here is what this could sound like: "Your partnership is so important to us and the (people, animals, environment) we serve. I appreciate you and want you to know that your passion to make a difference means so much to me. And I want to be sure you know that all of us at (organization name) are here to serve you and answer any questions or concerns you might have. So today, I'll be asking some questions to be sure I am aligned with you on what you want to accomplish through (name of your organization). I will also keep our meeting moving along so that we can cover everything we need to talk about in the time you've given me. Is that OK with you?"

Then *transition:* Ask permission, through a quick question, to move to the next part of your meeting. You are signaling a transition to being curious. Example: "I was touched to hear your story of XXX and how it inspired you to give. Would you mind me asking a few more questions about that?"

2. **Be Curious**— In this step you want to secure more information about what drives the donor to give and discover if she has questions about something you have already talked about. You want to ask open-ended questions (not Yes/No questions) to learn more. You are also letting the donor know you have HEARD her— "As we've talked the past several months, I've seen your concern for xxx. You've told me how you feel and why this matters to you. What are your thoughts now? OR Has this changed or developed in any way?" PAUSE.

Then continue to be curious— You want not only to be curious with great questions, but also to listen with your whole being. What is the donor saying, and what is her body language indicating? What does she seem worried or excited about?

Depending on where you are with the donor, some questions may sound like this:

- "I know you said that the major reason you are interested in X is Y. I was just wondering, how did you develop that interest?"
- "After reading over the proposal, what stood out to you, or do you have more questions about or want to learn more about something?"
- "Now that we've talked more about this project, what concerns do you have? What is still unclear? What would you like to learn more about?"

Then *transition:* Ask permission, through a quick question, to move to the next part of your meeting. You are signaling a transition to asking. Example: "You said earlier that the main reason you are interested in X is this. I want to tell you about how you can fulfill that interest. Is that OK with you?"

3. Ask— The objective here is to ask. Here you are asking the donor to take an action, to make a decision, to commit to giving. This needs to be short and said in one breath. Example: "Would you consider a gift of $x for Project X?" Keep it simple, clear, and concise – and then pause to let the donor respond.

Note that there is not more to say at this point because the majority of the work is what happened earlier in previous meetings and in these *align* and *be curious* steps. If you've done those correctly, the ask stage follows naturally.

There is a great deal of complexity that follows the asking step, in that there are all types of options the donor has that you will encounter once you have asked. And any one of those options will force you to go around the alignment circle a number of times in one conversation.

You may have to check in on whether the donor's interests are truly aligned with a project you are proposing, or questions she may have about the materials on the project you sent, or thoughts, concerns or objections about the project. Or she may say "no" or "maybe"— and that will have you circling around again.

Celebrate

When we were designing the Permission-Based Asking Model™ we all realized that a celebration point needed to be in the model. First, because thanking is not enough, and second, because even if the response you have received from the donor is a "no" or anything different from what you expected (or wanted), the best thing to do is honor and empower the donor by celebrating their personal choice and their independence.

If you stop to think about it, most of the material on asking that is out in the non-profit sector ends the process with a thank you. And that is good. But it doesn't celebrate the donor's choice and independence. And that's why we, and our team, feel this point is so important.

You could influence and pressure the donor to give out of obligation, and you might get a gift. But the long-term effect of that strategy is disastrous, as it violates the donor.

Think of how freeing it will be for the donor to be very comfortable in saying "no." What this does is keep the relationship intact, which is the most important value. Over and over again, we have seen donors treated with honor when they said "no" — and these same donors turn around and give again, and sometimes give transformationally. You need to value the long-term.

The objective of the *Celebrate* step in our asking model is to fill the donor's heart, mind and spirit with joy. In this phase you are providing information, stories and pictures that will drive satisfaction in the donor. When you leave the donor's presence you want her to experience significant joy in knowing that her decision to give was the right thing to do, and that great things are going to happen as a result. You need to share not only facts but also stories and pictures.

And if she decided not to give, or not to give now, or not to give as much as you asked—you want to leave her feeling honored, heard, and appreciated.

If the donor agreed to your ask, your comment back might sound like this: "Anita, thank you for being clear with me about where you are in relation to giving to this project. As your partner, knowing how you think about this is what is most important to me. It helps me serve you and keep you connected to what is most meaningful to you. I want you to know that this (your prepared outcome) will happen because of your gift."

Then you go on to explain in more detail how a life is going to be changed—how an animal will be saved, how a lake will be restored, etc.—and what this means to the people involved. Then you continue: "This is just amazing! I hope you can feel the joy, the restoration, the hope and the thankfulness coming your way."

If your donor did NOT agree, you will first be curious and ask great questions about where your donor is at this time. And then your comment back might sound like this: "You know, Jane, I completely understand what you are saying. And I want you to know that I celebrate and honor your decision not to get involved at this time. It is really important to me and the rest of the team at (name of organization) that you have a total sense of freedom to do what you need to do in your relationship with us. So many times, the fundraising thing is filled with obligation and pressure, and that is the last thing we want you to feel. In fact, later today or tonight when you think about this conversation, I want you to experience tremendous peace, calmness and comfort in knowing that all is well in our relationship. You have made a decision that is right for you, and I respect and honor that."

Of course, as you have been in the alignment circle with this donor, you have secured information about what the next step should be if the answer is "no." That should be part of your objective. If you are sensing a "no" coming, you should be curious about what the "no" means and therefore what the next steps should be.

The most important thing is to leave the donor with a full sense of worthiness, adequacy, calmness and satisfaction. You don't want her to feel like she has disappointed you or let you down. No—this is all part of a longer-term journey. Keep that in mind.

The Alignment Cycle Matrix

Some things stay the same. Other things change.

This is true in every relationship. That's why, when we designed the Permission-Based Asking Model™, we made it circular—so changes and nuances could be accommodated and handled.

This is a very important concept. Remember, your objective is NOT to get the money at all costs. Your objective is to satisfy and fulfill donor passions and interests AND do it in a manner that honors and respects the donor and her timing and circumstances.

This means you will need to listen carefully and modify your agenda every time you hear a response from the donor that is different than what you expected or wanted. This is difficult, we know. But it is so important. And if you are present to your donor and curious, you won't be asking questions to get an answer you want or expect or making assumptions about where your donor is.

You may slip up on this one, as that is the natural tendency—to press ahead toward the objective. But learn to be aware and catch yourself. Over time you'll get better at it. Here's the thing—the more neutral you can be, the less you will get caught off-guard or get tight and not be able to be creative and curious in your response. And you'll be more honoring and present to your donor.

The most common complaint we hear from donors is summed up in the phrase: "All they want is my money." This means that we (the collective non-profit community) have trained the donor population to expect to be badgered for money. It is in this culture and environment that we are asking you to be different. This means that you will practice real and authentic caring while you pursue the net revenue the organization needs.

The *Alignment Cycle* helps you do that. It keeps you going round and round, carefully and delicately handling the feelings, concerns, questions and wonderings the donor has. And to help you do that, we've created the **Alignment Cycle Matrix**, which outlines great questions you can use in your various donor meetings or situations that may come up.

As you use the concepts in the alignment process, remember that your objective is not to jump out of the alignment cycle and "get going." No. It is to keep going round and round, answering and dealing with the donor's questions and concerns until you feel it is natural to move on.

Dealing with Fear, Developing Conversation

"I was afraid."

It's a simple yet profound statement that we've all uttered.

I (Richard) had heart surgery recently—dealing with AFIB. I was afraid. While everyone said it was a normal procedure, all I could think about was leaving the planet. I was truly afraid.

But that's understandable. When you face potential death, most people are afraid.

But I've also said "I'm afraid" about conversations I had. So has Jeff. So have all of us. "I just didn't feel comfortable. I was afraid to go there."

This is normal.

That's why any writings about *asking* need to deal with *fear*.

When meeting with a donor, we all want to show up and be present, kind, confident, connecting and authentic. We prepare and practice, but on the way to the meeting we start feeling tight and anxious, we get butterflies in our stomach, and our heart rate increases. Why? Because our bodies automatically go into a "Fight, Flight, or Freeze" response when under stress.

It's a natural system in the body that has enabled humans to respond rapidly in order to cope with threats to survival. The amygdala is the part of the brain that initiates the fight or

THE ALIGNMENT MATRIX

Topic	Alignment Objective	Curiosity Questions
General Donor Information	To get to know the donor	What is your communication style & preferences?
		What brings you the most fulfillment in life?
		Who have been the most influential role models or mentors to you?
		What would you like to be remembered for?
Passions and Interests	To I.D. Passions and Interests	What are the most important things you'd like to accomplish this year?
		What inspired you to invest in our organization?
		What motivates you to continue to give?
		Why is our organization important to you?
		What would you like to see changed or improved?
Organization Understanding and Connection	To increase connection	How do you want to be involved?
		What would you like to know about us?
		Of our programs, what do you want to learn about the most?
		What event most interest you to attend?
Preparing the Ask	To prepare the ask	What is important to you in your giving decision process?
		Can you walk me through your decision making process?
		How do you like to be told about the results of your gift?
Resistance in the Gift Amount	To determine the right amount	Tell me more about what amount would work?
		What would make giving this amount work for you?
A Project Already Presented	To determine fit	What about this project is most exciting to you?
		How would you change it?
		What concerns do you have?
		Did this capture what you are trying to accomplish?
Reason Not to Give	To determine reason	Tell me more about your decision?
		What might we have done that didn't support your decision?
		What key factors influenced your decision?
		What do we need to change?
Maybe Give Later	To determine why and when	What questions are still unanswered for you?
		What concerns do you have?
		What do you still need to make a decision?
		When should I be back in touch with you?

flight response, and what is crazy about that is it can't distinguish between a real threat and a *perceived* threat. The fight or flight response is automatic, and responds the same way to an important donor meeting or to being chased by a tiger. So even though meeting with a donor isn't going to kill you, your amygdala responds as though it may.

Any kind of stress—the ding of a text message, email from a colleague, a challenge at work—can all trigger our reactive response. When the "fight, flight or freeze" response kicks in, what happens in a conversation is that *fight* is represented by actions that go against (argue, manipulate, talk more), *flight* is represented by actions that disconnect (avoid, space out, end the meeting quickly) or *freeze* (stick to a position, dig in, lack creativity). All these responses are the opposite of how we want to be with a donor.

So, our natural reaction to stress was and is great when we require it for survival, because it triggers hormones and our nervous system into narrow focus, hypervigilance, defensiveness, increased heart rate, and tension ready to spring. But when meeting with a donor, it takes away our ability to function in much-needed ways like big-picture thinking, confidence, creativity and calm presence.

Now you know why, when you're with a donor asking for a gift, you may start talking too much, bulldozing, feeling spacey, having a hard time concentrating, feeling tight and unable to be creative, or just wanting to give up and get out of there if it isn't going well. It's a natural automatic body reaction to stress.

What should you do?

1. **Be aware that you're in this state and tell yourself it's normal.** You're currently in your head, thinking you can just push this feeling away, and it's messing you up. Name what it is you're feeling—fear.
2. **Pause, take a breath.** Remember, the signs of reacting to fear are that you stop listening, you talk too much, you get tense and tight, you lose your train of thought and conversation, etc. So, noticing your shallow breathing and taking some longer breaths (particularly longer out-breaths) helps slow you down and gets you back to the present moment.
3. **Get back in your body.** Wiggle your fingers or toes and get back into your body. Why your body? Because the reaction

you are having is hormonal and chemical and is in your body.

4. **Remember what this is about**. Put your hand on your heart and say to yourself: "This is about the donor and her passions and interests. I'm here to help her find fulfillment and joy. This is not about the money. This is not about me."

5. **Get back into the alignment circle**. This is where you can intellectually check in and see where things are. And if they're not right, then go around the circle and it will be fine. You could say something like, "Yikes there I go again. I just realized I got overexcited and was talking way too much. What I really want to hear is where you are in all of this?" And if you can use self-deprecating humor in these situations where you have "lost it" that puts you and your donor at ease.

The other big thing you can do is continue to work on developing your asking language, which needs to be about open-ended questions rather than yes-or-no questions.

Here are a few ideas of what we are talking about:

- In thinking about email, the telephone, written correspondence, face-to-face meetings, social media, and so on—how would you describe your communication style and preferences?
- What has brought you the most fulfillment in your life?
- What are you most passionate about in your life right now?
- How did you decide to give your first gift?
- Why are you involved with our organization?
- How do you want to be involved?
- What would you like to know about us?
- Tell me more?
- Can you walk me through your decision-making process?
- What is important to you as you make decisions to give?
- Can you restate, in your own words, what you hope to

gain from successful completion of this program?
- What are the key factors that influenced you in making this decision?
- What questions are still unanswered for you?
- What concerns do you have?
- What do you still need to be able to decide?

Remember, always ask for permission. Remember that your interaction with your donor is circular, which is why you need to stay in the alignment circle until you find a natural place to exit. And always keep in mind that this major gift "thing" is never about the money. It is about walking with another human being and helping them fulfill their passions and interests.

Preparing to Use the Permission-Based Asking Model™—Five Steps to Take

Now that you have yourself fully anchored in The Permission-Based Asking Model™, we want to be sure you are prepared to use the model with a donor. And being prepared involves the following five steps:

1. Know your donor.
2. Know your program.
3. Make a perfect match of program to your donor.
4. Compose the ask.
5. Practice the ask.

Know Your Donor

"I'm going to get it out there and start asking my donors," the determined MGO said. And that's how she defined an important step in the success in raising major gifts money. Ouch! It is never surprising to us anymore to see MGOs jump right into asking their donor for a gift. It's not that asking is a bad idea— it's not. In fact, as we said earlier, asking is a central part of fundraising. But most asks are done very poorly. We looked carefully at the information out there on the subject of asking and—and guess what?—we disagree with about 80 percent of it. People who are aiming to teach others how to prepare an ask, a case for support or a proposal tend to place almost all their emphasis on the writing and ignore the preparation.

Often, the advice starts with a phrase like "create a need statement" or "establish a theme." This is important, but it's the wrong starting place. Because, of course, it should start with the donor, the most important part of the equation. You might have a well-written statement or a fully developed theme, but unless it's based on knowing what donors want, they won't fully engage.

The practice of creating an ask before thinking carefully about the desires of the donor is symptomatic of a deeply held belief that donors really don't matter—donors are secondary in the value hierarchy of all the people in the nonprofit, because they are simply a source of cash. Then what actually happens is that program and what you do becomes more important. And this is wrong. You can dream about the way to make change all day long, but even the most effective plan won't come off if you haven't thought first about who'd be interested in funding it. There are two questions you should ask yourself to help you get you off to a great start in knowing your donor:

1. Who is this donor?
2. What does she want and need in this relationship?

Google your donor. You'll likely find out about jobs, awards, assets, interests, and connections. If you're not a research person, perhaps someone can summarize each donor's life and interests for you. Follow every trail, because there's so much information in just this one source. Another good source of information is www.reference.com. If the donor is an attorney go to www.martindale.com for additional info. If a doctor, try www.ama-assn.org.

Do wealth and asset research. As of this writing, Wealth Engine and Blackbaud are good tools for wealth overlays and asset information. Other good sources include www.zillow.com, www.zoominfo.com, www.secinfo.com, and www.hoovers.com.

Research a donor's past giving, both to your organization and to others. The first part should be easy, but you'd be surprised how many MGOs don't have a running total of what a donor has given, when she gave, what her largest gift was, and notably, what inspired her to give each time. To find information about giving outside your organization, start with www.dsgiving.com or www.fec.gov or giving to your local political organizations, like this one from Virginia— https://www.vpap.org. If the person has a family foundation, get the 990 for the organization and see what gifts have been made. A great source for giving of all kinds is www.taxexemptworld.com. You'll be amazed by what you can learn.

Ask your donor! Your own intense curiosity is probably the best source of information you can have. When you're in contact with the donor, asking a lot of questions about her interests, inclinations, involvements and passions is a key to finding out what motivates her. Avoid focusing only on her interest in your nonprofit. Instead, find out what makes her tick. Asking the donor what she's interested in giving to in your organization may not, at first, yield as much information as asking what interests she pursues in all of her giving. The most successful fundraisers are those who can, over time, secure relevant information that will inform their unique approach to each donor. General and genuine curiosity and interest in the donor will yield far more information and trust than vaguely pecking away at what you think you want to know about how she perceives your organization.

You can't do enough to get to know your donor. There's nothing more important in the world of major gifts. And if you value your donors as partners—not as a source of cash—you'll naturally want to know them as you should.

Know Your Program

We're often amazed at how quickly some newly hired MGOs come to understand fully the programs of the organizations they serve. On the other hand, we're also often surprised at how many MGOs we meet who have been with an organization for five years, ten years, or even more, yet don't really have a clue.

Why the difference? Is it the type of person or the type of organization that explains the wide range of knowledge among MGOs about the programs they've been hired to represent? Could it be that the MGO who knows her program is the one who understands that her job is matching donor passions and interests to organizational needs and has been actively trained by the organization to know what it does? Maybe.

But what about the MGO who doesn't know the program at all? Putting the best light on it, maybe he expects others to know. Maybe he thinks someone else is charged with gathering the information and all he does is present it. Maybe these MGOs just don't grasp the big picture, which means they can't thoughtfully organize it for the donor. Could they be so busy with donor contact that they don't actually have any time to find out more about the charity?

Whatever the case, it's downright depressing when an MGO seems to know little about the program he represents. But it's an amazing thing to watch when someone gets it. It's exhilarating for the donor, the MGO, his manager, and the organization.

You can't expect to be successful as an MGO if you don't know your program. That's why, before you begin preparing for the ask, or scheduling any meetings where you want to ask for a gift, you need to take the following steps to make sure you're informed in this critical area:

▶ **Understand your organization's budget**. Spend time with your top finance person to gain a clear understanding of the organization's incoming and outgoing funds. Do you have any idea what the total expenditure is? What the total revenue is? What the major categories of each area are? If your answer is no, start finding out today.

▶ **Make sure you have agreement from management and administration that, if you can secure funding for a particular program or project that is in the budget, it is actually going to come about.** This sounds elementary, but this happens all the time. A donor wants to fund a budgeted program or project, but the program people don't really feel it is a priority. In other words, there is not alignment. The donor gives the money, and then nothing happens. Don't let this happen. Get agreement with all involved that this is definitely something everyone in the organization wants to move ahead on.

▶ **Dig for information about how each program category works.** This is about understanding the need being addressed, how the need is met, and the demographics of who is being helped—age, sex, race, marital status, social standing, you name it. If you don't understand this, how are you going to explain it to a donor? Yes, this does mean you'll have to read program plans and visit program sites. It also means taking time—quite a bit of time. When a new MGO starts, he should spend 30 to 40 percent of his time engaged in this activity alone because he needs to know his product to be effective. This part is the intellectual side of program knowledge. So, you need to work with program to ensure you have a solid, workable plan with a budget. Sound fundamental? It's not unheard of for rogue MGOs to promise all kinds of things to donors in order to get the gift, and only then ask the program people if they can pull it off. The poor donors must have been duped, because an accurate budget is a crucial element in letting them know how much to give, how their gifts are going to be used, and whether the organization has a long-term funding plan beyond their support. It's easy enough to say this project will cost $5 million over three years, but show the proof. As always, add the overhead to the project, to ensure every cost can be covered.

▶ **You also need to get into the emotional side of the program content**. No matter what the program is, whether helping people, the environment, animals, education, the arts—whatever what the cause—you must be emotionally connected to it. If your organization is helping the homeless, go sit with a homeless person and let that experience get into your heart. If you're helping animals, get into their world and feel it. If your program is about conservation, wander into the beauty and wonder of nature and marvel at it. If it's about cancer research, cry about the pain this dreaded disease has caused and fill your heart with hope for a solution. If it's about justice, be angry about how cruel and selfish people can be. Your heart must get engaged. You cannot stand outside of the emotional impact of your cause and hope to be an effective major gifts fundraiser. Fill your head with the program (engaging the intellect) and open your heart (engaging the emotions) to feel its impact on other people, the earth, and everything in it. Don't bypass this important step of engaging on both levels.

▶ **Gather stories and pictures that illustrate need and impact**. Remember that the role of an MGO is to experientially transport the donor right into the center of the problem the organization is addressing. If the MGO had a teleportation device, she could put donors in the middle of the action. They'd be able to hear, see, taste, and feel the experience. Until someone invents such a device, though, you must gather stories that take the donor to experience the sheer joy of seeing the need met. They should make you jump out of your chair and shout, "Wow! This is incredible!" If you can't picture yourself ever responding this way, that's OK. Sit for a while and ponder why. It'll be a good journey for you to take.

The programs at your nonprofit should be the center of the universe for your major gifts fundraising. It's the embodiment of the donors' passions, values, and interests. It's why they've joined you. They see a bit of themselves in your cause and are drawn in. So, embark on a journey to get yourself and them right in the middle of your organization's programs. Then stay there, constantly soaking it in, so you can always faithfully and truly represent it to your best donors.

Make the Perfect Match Between Program and Donor

"I have 150 donors on my caseload," said the frustrated and impatient MGO. "Do you really expect me to go through every single one and find a match between his or her interest and our program?"

Yes, we do. Every single one.

"But our donors don't have a single interest! They've just told me to use their gift where most needed."

What this actually means is, "I don't know what our donors' interests are."

That, in a few phrases, sums up one of the greatest problems in major gifts fundraising—the MGO doesn't know the passions and interests of the donors on her caseload. There are three common reasons for this:

1. *The MGO has been unable to connect with the donor.* This means there are donors on a caseload who aren't qualified, i.e. they haven't told the MGO they want to relate in a more personal way. So, why are they on the caseload? Giving a sum of money equal to or greater than the minimum criteria to be on a caseload is not a good enough reason. You need qualified donors on your caseload—but if they won't talk to you in person, by phone, e-mail, letter, fax or telegram, what's the point of keeping them on the caseload? If your job is to match donors' interests to the organization's work, and you can't find out their interests, you have to let them go. If, on

the other hand, you haven't really tried every avenue of contacting them, at every time it might be convenient for them, it's time to do that.

2. *The MGO hasn't asked the donor about his passions and interests.* There are several reasons. She hasn't gotten around to it. She doesn't know how to do it. She's uncomfortable asking about it. She doesn't think it's important. Or she honestly believes the donor has no specific interests. Whatever the reason, the fact remains that every donor does have an interest, and it's the job of the MGO to uncover it. If the MGO is too specific in the questioning process, it's much harder for the donor to answer. For instance, if the MGO asks, "What program interests you most?" she may not get an answer that works. If instead, she asks: "When you look at all of your giving, Ann, be it time or money, what captures your heart and your attention?" she may be more likely to get an answer—a trail she can then follow into her organization. The point is that we all have preferences for how we use our time and money. Your job is to, over time, work out how your donors like to use theirs.

3. *The donor isn't comfortable sharing this information.* The truth is that he isn't comfortable yet. The relationship needs to season and age. He needs to learn that you can be trusted with his thoughts and feelings. Give it time, but keep this line of questioning on your list of things to do. Keep learning in this critical area, and never give up trying.

Using the Permission-Based Asking Model™ will help you know what the donor is interested in and how you can match that interest to a program in your organization. But be careful how you do this. Here are some important principles to keep in mind:

1. *During the matching process keep an eye on the need for the organization to have undesignated funds.* If a donor is interested in helping younger children, there's a big difference

between asking the donor to help with a multifaceted children's program and asking them to fund the Thursday evening literacy classes on the West Side of Detroit between January and March. You'll obviously want to talk about all that detail, not only of that program but all programs. But your ask, while still staying in the donor's interest area, should be as general as possible. Be open with the donor about the need for the organization to have flexibility in its program spending. Donors always understand. They just want to know that their gifts will especially help those younger kids.

2. *If your cause involves helping people, find out who the donor wants to help in terms of gender and age.* Start with a gender match, then look for what age she prefers to help. Is it women? If so, old or young? Most donors will often be more likely to want to help a certain gender of a certain age. If your organization doesn't help people or develops some other cause, then move to Step 3.

3. *Look for sector (type of program) matches.* Is it education, shelter, work development, counseling, or protecting the environment? Including gender and age matches above, if relevant, find out what the donor wants to do. What does your donor get excited about?

4. *Try to determine the desired outcome of the match.* After you have imagined linking an individual donor with the program you think he'll love, visualize in advance whether the match seems satisfying. Spend a thoughtful moment considering how the donor will react to your suggested program. In your mind's eye, sit with the donor and propose what you've come up with as a place he can help. Is he thrilled? Has he found fulfillment and joy? If not, start over.

This is hard work. It takes time. But your donors are worth it. They're investing a good sum of money, so it's important to consider how carefully people weigh things before they buy.

To them and you, that transaction is a very sacred and special thing. Treat it with great care, as you would anything you value greatly in life.

Integrate Your "Presentation" into the Permission-Based Asking Model™

Now you are fully prepared. You have all the information you need. And it has taken a great deal of time. In fact, it takes more time and work to get ready for the ask than it does to actually create the ask itself. If you say, "I just don't have time to prepare," you are headed for trouble.

You have to spend time getting to know the donor, getting to know the program and matching the donor to the program before you can effectively use the asking model. This advance work isn't just casual activity an MGO does on the side. It's a very serious part of his job, one that requires an investment of time and effort, and it's just as important as any other responsibility.

Most asking fails because the MGO has just not put the effort into gathering the needed information. Now it's time to integrate all your knowledge and preparation into the asking model.

Here are six areas you need to be ready to address:

1. **Be ready to acknowledge past giving and interest.** There's nothing more satisfying to a donor than to be thanked for his giving and to be affirmed that what he is interested in is also what the organization is interested in—that there is a solid partnership between the two parties. This affirmation of the match creates a bond between the donor and the organization, a special link that confirms to the donor that she made the right decision in giving. Before you even get into using the asking model you need to know this information.

2. **Be ready to clearly state the need and the consequences of needs not met.** It is often difficult for many nonprofit insiders to state the need the charity is organized to meet in a compelling and emotional way. That's because they

haven't thought about it or are afraid of saying out loud just what the horrible consequence will be if the need is not met. Let's face it, most human need is not pretty. It can be incredibly sad—even hard to stomach, so there's no use in dressing it up. But, before you use the asking model you need to be ready with this important information.

3. **Be ready to state what you're going to do.** This is the part of the conversation with your donor that has to do with the program, and it needs to be specific, logical and caring. Most program write-ups for an ask or a proposal are filled with so much technical jargon that they don't grab the donors' hearts. Include plenty of description and human detail. Keep it simple and to the point. And when you read what you've written, ask yourself, "Can I honestly say this solves the problems presented in the need I've outlined above?" If not, don't move on until you can.

4. **Be ready to talk about the impact the donor's gift will have.** Prove that the gift will achieve what you say it will by showing ways the organization has been successful in the past in this very area. Tell stories and show pictures of the impact you've already had. Remember, Step 3 above only reveals half of the story—telling what you'll do, not the difference that the donor's action will make. Think of it in terms of the potential donor considering a purchase. Donors are buying something from you. They're buying the result of your work. They want the impact. You need to affirm their belief that if they give they actually will solve the problem.

5. **Be ready to provide clear budget details.** Be sure to include all the costs, including overhead, not only of the project itself but also an allocated portion of your organization's overhead. Don't pretend overhead doesn't exist or is smaller than it actually is.

6. **Be ready to describe the gift plan.** Lay out a clear and

simple plan for the donor on how you propose she will respond financially. You may be asking for a single gift, or a series of gifts over time, or a combination of cash and non-cash gifts, or a combination of any of the above, including any ways the donor suggests she would like to be involved. The plan is a forward-looking, long-term thing. Frankly, the concept of encouraging one annual gift is a poor approach, because it ties the organization and the donor to a specific time. The gift plan focuses the donor on the solution to a problem that needs solving now. There's a huge difference. The gift plan is far more satisfying to a donor than meeting a time-specific quota.

You are almost ready to use the asking model. Now it's time to practice.

Practice the Ask

Practicing for the ask helps you check if you are properly prepared. Here are three things to think about that will help you effectively practice for the ask and check how prepared you are:

1. Practice, practice, practice. Do you think you can wing it? You can't.

- Practice your ask presentation with your colleagues. Pretend your colleague is the donor, and speak directly to her.
- Have your colleague ask all the potential questions and find holes in your knowledge to ensure you anticipate these in the actual meeting.
- If more than one person is attending clarify roles and responsibilities. Also, set an agreement on how to get the other person back on track.
- Have all your facts and figures right.
- Prepare for every eventuality.
- Be sure you have a good story and that the emotional impact is there. Then, two days later, come back and do it again.

- Practice the model to the point that it feels natural.

2. *Relax.* On the day of the ask make sure you have all your materials, and that everyone is clear on their roles. Then, sit down with the donor, relax and demonstrate how he can change the world. If you've done all your work, you have every reason to succeed.

3. *Be comfortable with the fact that all of this takes time.* MGOs often are in a huge rush to just get to the ask. Chasing revenue like a $10 bill blown away by the wind, they skip over all the steps we've written about above and wonder why the donor turned them down. A good ask takes a lot of preparation. And a lot of preparation takes a lot of time. Donors see this, appreciate it and respond to it. They see how much time and passion you've invested. It's a passion they share, so when they see it, they'll respond. Embrace the work it takes.

If you prepare with these three points in mind and are a true partner and facilitator using the asking model, your donor will feel honored, known, and cared for in this important conversation asking for a gift.

Making the Ask

Once you feel ready to ask and you've scheduled a meeting, ease into the meeting using the Permission-Based Asking Model™ we described earlier in this chapter. Be sure you don't deliver a prepared speech word for word, but have an outline as a guide. We also recommend having a list of questions prepared that you feel comfortable using as you look to be curious and learn more about your donor's passions and interests and readiness to give. Listen carefully for responses or flags that signal the donor is more interested in certain aspects. Be agile enough to respond accordingly.

Ask questions to keep the donor engaged and to measure his interest: "Did I explain that adequately?" "How do you feel about that idea?" "What ideas do you have?"

Now that you have explained the project or goal, be clear, concise and precise in conveying the ask amount. Say something like "I am asking for your commitment of, or we seek your consideration of a gift of, or we are seeking your leadership in, or to further our shared vision through..."

Whatever way you say it, after asking for a specific amount for a specific outcome, pause. Wait for the donor to respond. It could be an enthusiastic "Yes!" But more likely, he won't want to make an immediate commitment and may even say something along the lines of "no."

Or, he might have one or more concerns. But if you clearly know what the donor wants from the giving transaction and you have prepared well, you will likely have a positive answer—one that will bring great joy to the donor and will provide resources for your organization.

Are you still wondering how the ask should be worded? You won't have to wonder if you know what the donor wants out of the giving transaction, have a solid relationship built on trust and openness and use the Permission-Based Asking Model™ as your guide. In other words, you will already know what she wants and how she communicates before you make the ask. No expert can tell you how to relate to a friend.

Handling Your Donors' Concerns and Questions

We all know it can be challenging when you have worked very hard on your preparation, think a donor is ready to give, and then they don't say yes. Our tendency, in this situation can be to take it personally, stumble, become anxious, defend, or fear failure. But a donor's response is nothing more than a signal or marker of where they are in this moment. And the minute you hear one, instead of turning inward and becoming depressed or anxious, the best thing you can do is be curious.

Most everyone in the fundraising sector talk and write about *objections* to your cause, organization, project, amount requested, timing, and you. If you are using the Permission-Based Asking Model™ all along the way in your donor conversations, you should already be pretty clear about what your donor connects to and cares about in your organization. You know their passions and interests and the cause that they hold dear, and in your Permission-Based Asking conversation, you will know if a project you are proposing is of interest before you ever ask them for a gift. And in all of these conversations, you are building a partnership of trust. If you still feel you don't connect at all to a donor you can decide if you are the right MGO to be managing them. So, what does that leave when it comes down to actually asking for a gift? It leaves mostly amount and timing.

Here's another thing about the word *objections*. For some of us, that word doesn't hold a lot of emotion and it works fine. For others, it brings with it feeling that something is wrong, that the donor isn't cooperating, that you have failed, makes you feel tight and nervous, and makes the focus on this having to be a yes. The focus needs to be on fulfilling the donor's passion and interests. So, we have started using the word response instead of the word *objection*. Because they are just responding to where they are in the moment, that is all.

When the MGO learns from the donor where the hesitation or concern is really coming from, she can gently work through it with the donor. So, as you hear a response that is not an automatic yes, try to figure out which of these reasons apply to your situation. Then remember this is an opportunity, to increase your understanding of the donor's circumstances, empower your donor, and build a more trusting relationship. Upon hearing their response, do the following:

1. Listen and ask. Before you respond in any way, it helps a great deal if you can properly understand it and the thought and emotion behind it. Find what lies at the root. This requires that you listen more, ask more questions, and seek out the background and detail of their response. Seek to read between the lines to find out the emotion behind it. The surface response may not be the whole story. Keep the conversation going to pull out the real reason and clarify the details. This not only uncovers the real reasons behind their response, it shows that you're personally interested in the donor's concerns. It builds trust and enables you to elevate the conversation to a joint problem-solving conversation instead of a sales situation where you're on the spot. Here are some ideas to help you do this:

- When you hear the response, repeat it. "That sounds like a lot of money." Then pause and hear what more they have to share. Remember pausing gives them some space to think and process.

- Restate it as a question. "You shared that this is a lot of money?" Then pause and hear what more they have to share.

- Ask the donor to share more. "Tell me more about that."

- Summarize and ask for more: "It sounds like you have several concerns here related to being able to manage this size gift all at once. What else concerns you?"

- Don't start offering solutions until you have fully explored and understand why they gave the response they gave.

- Ask them for solutions before you start offering ones. What might work better for you? Is there better timing than now? How might breaking down this gift into smaller segments work better for you?

2. Accept the person and where they are. Once you've discovered it, the next stage is to acknowledge not only the response, but the person as well. First and foremost accept the person, show you value him and ensure he knows that he has every right to not say yes at this time.

All of this can be done without words and through attitude. Saying no can be a scary act, and people can fear your responses. Remember, this is stressful for your donor too and they go into their own stress response. By not reacting negatively, by accepting the no, the not right now, or the lower amount, you also accept and honor the person. By doing this, you build both his trust and his sense of connection with you. Your main goal here is to seek to understand the reason the donor isn't saying yes at this time.

Your donor might say something like, "Wow, we love your mission and this project, but my oldest just went to college and the economy has taken a chunk out of my savings." Be present to your donor in this moment and don't just assume she won't be able to do anything until her child is out of college. Ask questions. Ask about her child's college and interests. Ask what timing would work. Suggest ways to break down the project into smaller giving amounts. Keep telling her how her gift makes a difference and keep building the relationship.

It also means accepting the additional work that addressing the response will require of you. Once you're clear on the reasons for the response, what do you do? Be prepared to investigate other offers, revise your plan, follow up with the donor on other opportunities or with a synopsis of your conversation…whatever you need to do to deepen the relationship with the donor and honor their decision after the meeting. Remember, you need to focus on the long-term even if the immediate answer is a no.

The great thing is in the asking model you return to align before you celebrate. Even if you have not come up with a clear decision on the giving you summarize the conversation and always have a next step both you and the donor agree on.

3. Consider these facts in all of your dealings with donors. Here's a list of what donors believe were the reasons they thought the MGO was not effective in his contact with the donor. These are actual quotes:

- The MGO didn't show that she was interested in getting my donation.
- He failed to call or follow up with me in any way.
- There wasn't an introductory and personal paragraph to the

e-mail he sent. It seemed like a generic communication.
- There wasn't a call to action.
- She didn't really know me or what I was interested in (read: didn't qualify).
- He didn't learn about my timeline.
- She never talked with me about money. He never asked what I wanted.
- She didn't uncover any compelling reasons why I would give.
- He didn't appear to care.
- She didn't attempt to develop a relationship.

When a donor does not enthusiastically say yes to fulfilling his passions and interests through the offer you've developed, know this is simply not the right fit at this time. Embrace them, honor their decision, and look for the real meaning. That meaning will lead you to the place you need to be in your relationship with the donor.

Remember: In every scenario, your meeting with a donor should end in celebration. Even if you don't get an immediate yes, the donor has still made a significant impact in the community by partnering with your organization. Saying no, maybe, not now, or not that much is just as difficult for the donor to say as it is for you to hear, if not more difficult for the donor. Ending the meeting with an acknowledgement of the difference they are making in the world is the positive note that will help you to continue to grow that relationship moving forward.

Asking is a very complex part of the relationship. By taking the time to prepare for asking for a gift using the Permission-Based Asking Model™ as your philosophical guide, you will be able to follow steps that will keep your donor at the center of your focus, and help you to honor the donor no matter what the result of the meeting may be.

And the donor, being kept at the center, and empowered to

be a true partner, will engage at higher levels, wanting to fulfill their passions and interests vs giving you a gift out of obligation or to make you go away. That is where the magic is. Where the spiritual experience of giving happens. That is where making a difference in the world fills up your donors' heart with purpose and hope. This is what makes all the work you do every day worth every second of it!

Pause for Thought:
A Success Story
Richard Perry

The call came around 10:30 in the morning. The MGO I was in touch with could barely contain herself, and I could hardly understand what she was saying. Her tone was electric. "I can't believe it!" she cheered, and then proceeded to tell the story of her meeting with a donor earlier that morning.

"I went into the meeting feeling very nervous and wondering if I'd prepared properly," she told me. But as she carefully went through the points we've described on the previous pages, she could tell that the donor was really resonating with everything she said. Her statements of gratitude for the donor's past giving, the way she'd matched the donor's interests to the organization's need, her articulation of the immensity of the need and the way in which her gift could help to provide a solution—it all flowed smoothly. There was hardly any question she was unprepared to answer. Then it happened.

"Richard, suddenly, the donor asked me a question that I wasn't quite ready for," she said.

"What was that?" I asked.

"She asked how much money I wanted her to give. My heart was pounding! And for a minute I just didn't know what to say. Then I remembered the work I had done preparing for this meeting. Although I hadn't been prepared for the donor to just come out and ask me this question, I knew the answer. So, I told her what I was thinking. I said, 'A million dollars!' I just said it!"

Well, by this time I was gnawing on the side of my desk in anticipation, but I let her enjoy the thrill of the pregnant pause.

Finally, I heard the news.

"She said YES! My donor said yes! She was practically screaming into the phone. One million dollars, Richard! Can you believe it?"

"Yes, I can," I said. "And here's why I can believe it. You were prepared. You were focused on your donor and her desires. You knew where you were going and exactly where you were going. And what mattered most to you was not the money but all the joy the donor would experience by helping in this generous way and all the help people in need would get. These are all the reasons this worked for you."

After we hung up, I sat for a few minutes and thought about what had happened. I was elated. I marveled at how, once again, a person with great wealth and ability had been partnered with a caring MGO. I reflected on how that union had released huge amounts of needed resources into our world, and how those resources would now be flowing out to ease people's pain, heal their wounds, save their lives, and restore their hope. What a wonderful thing! What a humbling event. What a miracle that we can actually be part of something so precious and special. I am truly amazed every time this happens. And whether the gift is a million dollars or ten, it is still a very sacred and extraordinary moment.

Stop for a moment to take in this extraordinary chain of events:

1. One human being opens her heart and hands to place her love and care into the hands of another person, the MGO whom she has come to trust and believe in.
2. That love and care is then channeled to people in need.
3. The people in need are transformed, blessed, renewed.

In that series of events, something powerful, magical, and mystical has happened to everyone involved.

Can life get any better? As you think about writing the perfect proposal, I hope you've been able to see how important it is to prepare and listen well. When you truly listen to the donors and then work hard to deliver their heart's desire, so many good things happen. And we all need a lot of good things to happen these days—in our own lives and in the lives of those around us.

Chapter 11: Managing UP

As a major gift fundraiser, you may be asked to manage the donor portfolio of your manager, CEO or Executive Director (ED). In order to be effective, you have to have the ability to "manage up." Managing up means that you are working with your CEO, ED or DoD to cultivate, steward and solicit a small caseload of donors by managing their time, keeping them on track and telling them what they need to do with each of their donors.

Now, many MGO's we've worked with are hesitant about this because they find it intimidating to tell their boss what to do. But, any good manager or leader of a non-profit will welcome and want someone under them to help them manage their caseload of donors.

Not allowing you to "manage up" will set leaders up for failure. We have seen it too many times. CEO's who commit to working 25-50% of their time and it's nowhere near that. This is why good leaders let YOU manage them.

The whole reason to manage up is because YOU are the only one that is really thinking about your major donors all the time. That doesn't mean leaders don't care about donors, it's just that they have so much going on, that they need YOU to lead on the cultivation, stewardship and solicitation of the donor to be effective.

It also means that you are working with leadership to help you solicit your own donors. The only way to do that effectively is to take control of the major gift portfolios, put it on your shoulders and make it as easy as possible for leadership to help you succeed.

The key to managing up is not to assume that anyone in leadership is being proactive about their own caseload. They are way too busy. This is your job – your responsibility. And the only way this works is if you have the mindset that nothing will happen unless you lead on it.

How do you do this practically? Here are some ideas for you:

▶ Sit with leadership and make sure they agree to how you will manage their portfolio. Make sure they agree that you will be "telling" them what they need to do and following up to make sure it gets done—remember good leaders love that you will be managing their moves.

▶ Then, let leadership understand how your relationship with them will work. This means, telling them that you will help them set goals, create a 12-month strategic plan, tier the donors and work with them ongoing to help them manage the day to day by meeting with them frequently.

▶ Consider their caseload of donors as if it's yours—meaning you're looking ahead and communicating to leadership what THEY NEED to do. Good leaders want you to tell them what they should do. They don't have the time to think about it. It's up to you to lead on it and anticipate next moves.

▶ Set up a reoccurring meeting (We like weekly because they will cancel half the meetings) where you go over specific moves with donors, discuss in-depth strategy for specific donors and talk about the action items needed in the next week. This is critical to keeping them on track.

- In reviewing your own caseload, look months ahead to when you anticipate your leadership's involvement in soliciting your donors and get it on their schedule. Don't surprise your CEO, ED or DoD at the last minute saying you need them to come on a donor solicitation visit. That will not go over well. The key is planning way ahead.

- Always be thinking of personal touchpoints to recommend to leaderships caseload. You need to know them almost as well as the CEO does.

- Make sure you receive the daily gift report for their donors. It's very important that you "look out for" any of leadership's donors (including your portfolio of donors) to properly thank in a timely manner.

- Put all of your future moves or tasks in your calendar or database. This will help you stay on top of what needs to be done every day and help you remind leadership what they need to do.

- Hold an annual review of the portfolio with the leader. Go over each donor, remove those that need to come off and bring on new donors. Evaluate the year and talk about what you want to accomplish in the year ahead. This meeting will help you develop your next year's strategic plan for your leader.

Cultivating, stewarding and managing your own donors is tough enough. Managing up requires that you stay on top of the planning, goal setting and daily moves for your leader in order to help them be successful. And, if they're successful. So are you.

Chapter 12:
Closing the Circle:
Thank Yous, Reporting Back, and Accountability

With all the research that's been done, all the articles that have been written, and all the attention the topic gets at every fundraising conference, you might think that thanking donors would be something that comes naturally for nonprofits. Unfortunately, that is not the case—and that's why we have to address it here.

The Importance of Thanks

Thanking a major donor (or any donor for that matter) is crucial if you ever want another gift from that donor again. And, as we said, you would think this is a "no brainer" for nonprofit's but they fail over and over again. Let us tell you a story we heard recently from an executive director of a nonprofit.

During the holidays this particular organization received a $25,000 gift from one of their major donors. The gift was processed immediately to put into the bank of course, but for some reason it was never acknowledged…by anyone. No receipt, no letter, no phone call from the executive director, Jim (not his real name. Not good).

Six months later Jim is having coffee with a donor and he looks over and sees another major donor of his sitting near them. The ED goes over to the table and greets him. The donor is pleasant, but then asks him, "Jim, just wondering if you received my $25,000 gift last Christmas. I never got a receipt for it." (Now, of course the donor knew they did get it because he saw it come out of his account).

Jim was extremely embarrassed and promised the donor to find out what happened. Then the donor offered this. "Jim, I don't want you to feel too badly. When I sent you that gift of $25,000 I also sent the same amount to 8 other organizations. I only received a letter of thanks from one of them. It was from a small soup kitchen in my state run by two people. I decided next year I will be sending them the whole $200,000…so, you're not the only organization that failed to send me a thank you letter."

That hit Jim right in the gut. After investigating what happened at his organization and how a $25,000 gift was not acknowledged they found a glitch in their whole system and procedures. It makes me wonder what happened with the other six organizations that failed to thank that donor.

So, the lessons learned here are:

- ▶ Make sure you have the proper systems, procedures and protocols in place to quickly acknowledge a gift… especially a major gift. A good rule is to have a thank you letter out within 48 hours of receiving it.

- ▶ Along with getting out the letter, make sure your protocols include how donors are thanked based on their gift amount. This will be different for every organization, but not all gifts will JUST get a letter of thanks. A large gift may also get a call from the VP of development, a larger gift will warrant a call from the executive director or even the board chair. The point is to set up a system where everyone understands what to do for any type of gift and its written down and codified.

▶ Donors care about being thanked. A few development directors have actually told me, "Well, our donors really don't like to be thanked. They are just humble people." What? Don't think that for a minute. Thank, thank, thank.

Thanking Properly

The basic thank you procedure as we noted above includes an official receipt, a letter from the executive director and based on the size of the gift, a phone call from within the organization. Beyond that, it really is based on how well you know the donor and what the expectations are from the donor.

In other words, if a donor gives a sizable gift of five, six or 7 figures, obviously there are potential naming rights, public recognition on a "donor wall" and other public and private ways to thank a donor that is MEANINGFUL to a donor. That is the key. Some donors may not want public recognition. Honor that request. Others might want all of their family and friends to be part of a celebration of a gift. The key is to find out from the donor what they are comfortable with.

We have seen too many organizations mess this up. Either they "under thanked" or "over-thanked a donor and it just didn't go well. Thanking a donor properly after receiving a gift is one of the most important cultivation efforts for the next gift. So make sure your organization understands this.

Other Types of Thanking

Another way to thank a donor is to "surprise them" when they least expect it. Great donor cultivation always includes activities that will stand out in the donor's mind and heart. Think about it. When a donor gives a gift, they expect to get a thank you. However, they don't expect a personal handwritten note from you that just says how grateful you are for their support. Those unexpected thank you's stick with your donor. Here are some practical ideas:

1. Every day write 5 personal thank you notes to donors on your caseload.
2. Call 3 donors every day to show your organization's gratitude.
3. If you are "in the field" send a postcard from that area to some of your donors telling them how grateful you are for their support.
4. Have your executive director or President send personal notes and make phone calls to five donors every week.

We think you get the idea. Thank the donor when they are happily unaware. It will make a big impact on them and their future giving.

Reporting Back

We think if there is one thing that we get worked up the most about it is when organizations do not report back how a donor's gift made a difference. When a nonprofit doesn't tell a donor how their gift made an impact they are holding the donor in contempt. Yep, that is pretty strong, but it needs to be because nonprofits are absolutely failing at this.

Note the chart on the next page. This is the cycle of communication for a donor. First, you make them aware of a need. The donor responds by giving you a gift. Then you thank the donor, and tell the donor how their gift made a difference. If you miss that last important step, your chances of receiving another gift is almost nil.

Donors respond positively when they know they actually had an effect on making a positive change or preventing a negative outcome. It's your job to tell them. And, here is the beauty of all this for your organization. Most nonprofits do such a poor job of this that if YOU can put the time, effort, and resources in it your organization will be far ahead of other organizations.

You see, unfortunately donors have come to expect so little of nonprofits that to actually do a great job of reporting back will leave an impression and that will be etched into their hearts.

Here are some ideas to let donors know they have made a difference:

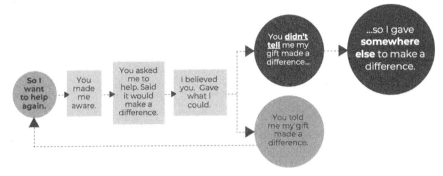

- ✔ Personal reports—if a donor gives to something specific make sure you write up a 6- and 12-month update report on that program or project. Work with program to make this happen.

- ✔ Newsletters—if your organization produces a regular newsletter, produce a personal letter or note to go with it and send it directly to your donor. This is a great way to use something that is mass produced but make it personal.

- ✔ Social media—technology is so wonderful because you can easily and cheaply report back to donors and make a lasting impact at the same time. Think about this for a minute: Let's say your organization builds water wells in Africa. Your program person is there when the first gush of water comes out of that well and takes a video of it with his iphone. He has the twitter, text, e-mail and facebook addresses of the donors who made that water well happen. Right there, minutes after that event happens, he can deliver that video. Now, the donor, sitting at a coffee shop in Chicago receives a text with a link to a video showing water coming out of that well. She sees the people jumping for joy and then the program person says to that donor, "you made this happen." How powerful is that?

- Annual Reports—this is another mass document that you can personalize highlighting specific programs that the donor funded.

- Annual board meetings—we like it when organizations can invite donors to at least one board meeting a year which focuses on what all has been done that year. It's a great way to report back and honor donors.

- Quarterly conference calls—some organizations we know hold quarterly conference calls for their major donors to update them on the work in the field. Again, another great touchpoint and an opportunity for donors to ask questions.

There are so many more ways to get creative to tell your donors they made a difference. The point is that your organization, if it wants to continue to grow the major gift program will have to invest people and resources into creating a dynamic "reporting back" culture. If you can help create this environment, you will see continued greater donor loyalty and revenue.

Be Accountable

Accountability seems like a harsh word. And for those of us who are independent spirits the word can evoke negative feelings. This is too bad. Because accountability is a good thing. It helps us do what all of us—managers and employees—want to do.

But often, management does not have their act together on the accountability thing. And this problem starts with managers not defining anything for their employee. We find this happens more often than not—where an employee is hired to do a job, but everything about the job, including the description and the objectives are so vague that no one understands what needs to be done.

Richard shares this story about meeting with a MGO about the way her manager related to her.

"I was shocked when the MGO closed the door and said, 'No one ever asked me for a goal for the year. In fact, I didn't even have a work plan. My job description was vague and general. And listen to this, my manager hardly ever checked in to see how things were going.'

"That conversation happened quite a few years ago. And, as time has gone on, I have become less shocked—actually, numbed—to the reality that management and accountability don't seem to matter much in the fundraising world. Believe it or not, management of a process and people is as important as getting the money for program. But you would never know it by looking at the inner workings of many nonprofits today!"

Unfortunately, there seems to be little value placed on setting goals, measuring progress against those goals and holding people accountable to do good and effective work. Good folks often work to help people or change the world through really good programs but often are stymied while money is lost, labor is wasted, laziness is rewarded and a lot of mindless activity is being tolerated. Organizations spiral down because employees who want to do good work get the nagging feeling that there's a gap between what's expected of them and what they can actually deliver. That gap—such a nasty little gap—is what will tear them down.

That's why it's so important for a kind and friendly management process and person to come alongside staff members and get rid of the gap so they're performing as expected. Management and accountability are not punitive and negative things— although many managers use them that way, to their shame and discredit.

Management and accountability systems and processes should be a kind, honest, direct way of helping a person meet expectations—not just management expectations, but their own expectations as well as those of their peers and subordinates. When management and accountability are done right, it's helpful, not hurtful. When it is, it's beautiful, because every person on the team has a chance to meet expectations. Both the team and the individual can succeed.

Without good management and accountability, leaders will not lead as they should, MGOs will not perform as they should, and the funds for program will not come in as they should. Our philosophy and approach to management and accountability is quite simple:

First, there has to be an economic destination for the team and each MGO. Call it a goal. Second, support needs to be given to individual MGOs so they can:

- ▶ Focus on caseload, not prospecting: Love the donor you have, not the one you can possibly get.
- ▶ Target retention of donors first, then upgrading.
- ▶ Relate to donors on caseload as individuals, not clusters or a group.
- ▶ Keep learning how to deal with donors' objections.
- ▶ Keep learning how to structure asks and proposals.
- ▶ Value, understand and report on their performance in a positive, constructive and honest way.

Third, management reporting needs to happen in five areas:

1. How the same donors are performing year to year. This is about retention of the donor, retention of the value the donor is giving and upgrading.
2. How those donors are performing against individual goals.
3. How many visits, contacts and asks the MGO is making.
4. Unusual gains and losses for any donor on the caseload to make sure other numbers are not being skewed.
5. How the MGO is performing generally.

Just do this kindly and positively, and you'll have happy, effective and productive MGOs. Happy, effective and productive MGOs equal happy donors. Happy donors means programs receive funding, which is what we all set out to do in the first place.

Chapter 13:
Heed These Critical Indispensables

If you've come this far in this book, you've learned tons about creating a culture of philanthropy in your organization that will support a robust major-giving program, as well as how to create and refine that program to ensure success. You've learned how to hire and train well, and how to nurture and empower your employees, especially your MGOs. If you're an MGO, you've learned how to hone your own skills.

Lots of good information so far but some of the concepts count as what we call indispensable and, as such, bear emphasizing and elaborating.

Refine That Job Description

Stop right now and pull out a copy of the MGO current job description. Then answer the following questions:

1. *Is the title donor-centered or organization-centered?* If it's Director of Major Gifts, Major Gifts Manager, Special Gifts Manager, Financial Development Director or something to do with money, major gifts, developing finances etc., then it's wrong. If it's Donor Relations Director, Manager of Donor Relations, or even Constituent Relations—something along

those lines—then it's right. Fundraising is all about the donor. Period. And there's something disturbing about handing a donor your business card that says something about major gifts, special gifts, financial development etc. It's wrong because it immediately tells the donor that what your MGO is about is getting his money. And by now, we hope, you know that this whole major gifts thing is not just about the money. It's about helping the donors express what they want to do in our hurting world through your organization.

2. *Is the statement of purpose or the primary objective in the job description solely about working with a group of assigned and qualified donors?* If not, there's trouble. As their manager if you've given your MGO more to do than work with a group of assigned and qualified donors then you don't understand the economics of major gifts fundraising. The very best investment the organization can make is to not add any other responsibilities to an MGO's job description. The very best ROI (Return on Investment) a fundraising manager can have is a MGO managing a group of assigned and qualified donors—and nothing else.

3. *Does the job responsibilities section have fewer than five categories of work?* How can one person be responsible for so many different things and be successful? As a manager, once a year get away with the organizational chart, take each job from the top down and list the five major categories of work for each. Start with the top job and work down as you keep delegating responsibility and limit yourself to five categories of work for each person. The job description for an MGO should have the following categories: manage an assigned and qualified group of donors (this includes stewardship and solicitation); qualify more donors as needed for caseload; relate to program personnel to secure information for donors; relate to team members (this is about belonging to a development team); and perform other duties as required. But

please don't use this final catch-all to add responsibilities that distract the MGO from her core work.

4. ***Does the job description have an accountability section?*** One of the most tragic and damaging mistakes in management is failing to tell an employee how his or her performance will be evaluated and measured. And this abusive situation is status quo for most organizations, large and small, around the world. We've seen job descriptions where a development director is charged with raising $30 million to $75 million, and there is not one clue as to how that person will be evaluated. If he raises it, does he keep his job? If he doesn't, is he fired? What if he raises more? This is a recipe for a lot of hurt, pain, anger and disillusionment. The accountability section of a very good job description will mirror each of the major categories of work in the responsibility section and describe how performance in each will be regularly and fairly judged.

The underlying values behind these guidelines are twofold: caring for donors and making sure the MGO knows what is expected. How does your job description—or the job descriptions you create for your staff—measure up?

Value Administrative Support

Why is it that so many MGOs suffer without proper support when smart leaders and managers know that delegating work and having support to get that work done is the most efficient and effective way to reach their objectives? There could be several explanations:

1. Organization leaders really don't know that there is huge potential in the donors that the MGO is managing. So why not just have her do other things?

2. They know there's huge potential, but they don't really believe the MGO can harvest it. So why waste the money on hiring support?

3. They are hands-on workers, so they avoid delegating and division of labor even when it could increase their own efficiency—and expect others to do the same.
4. They are financially conservative and risk-aversive, so adding labor that doesn't seem to contribute directly to raising more money feels counterintuitive.
5. They just don't understand the economics of keeping higher-cost employees focused on the duties that can earn the organization the most.

It could happen for any reason, but it seems to be mostly a lack of understanding of the economics of nonprofit fundraising. Obviously, if you're in a "solo shop" where you have to do everything and your major gifts caseload is only, say, 40 donors with an average annual donation of $2,500 each and little capacity to give more, then it might be difficult to argue that it makes sense to spend money on administrative support.

But what if that 40-donor caseload could, through proper management and cultivation, grow to 70 donors with an average annual value of $5,000 each, and with 10 of those having substantially greater potential? In that case, you should add a support person right away! There's enough economic potential to move the current annual value of $350,000 to $500,000 or $600,000; the only thing holding it all back is the MGO having the time to do it.

One MGO wrote us recently saying she needed to build a case with her board and executive director to show income would increase by adding administrative support. Here's a formula she— and you—could use to make that case.

> ✔ **Estimate how much past donor revenue has been lost because the MGO lacks time to cultivate donors.** To do this, take the total number of donors lost over the past two years but subtract those who have passed away, moved away with no forwarding address, or told you of their change in interest. You can reasonably conclude

that any others were lost because they didn't feel they were making a difference. The MGO didn't have time to tell them because she was too busy stuffing envelopes, setting up tables and chairs for an event that was revenue neutral, or performing other tasks someone insisted on. Just add up the lost revenue and share what you find.

✔ **Calculate potential caseload revenue that could be secured if the MGO had the time.** Uncover the total annual value of your current caseload by simply adding up how much each donor on the caseload gave last year. Let's say that your total is $600,000. Now multiply that number by 30 percent to 40 percent, bringing it to $180,000 to $240,000. This is the range of additional revenue you could get if you had the time to spend quality time with your donors. You'd be upgrading many donors efficiently and still have time to secure much larger gifts from the few who have great potential.

Now, if you total those two numbers together—the money lost and the potential not earned—you'll arrive at a tidy sum, and a good manager would see it provides room for administrative support.

We know you're thinking there's no way you can get 30 percent or 40 percent more revenue from your caseload. But the reason we used those numbers is precisely because that's exactly what we've seen in numerous past situations when an MGO's time was freed up by more administrative support.

One MGO successfully argued the case for more support, using the points above. She secured the administrative help, and the next year a donor who'd been giving $5,000 a year gave $1 million. Another who had been giving $2,500 a year gave $350,000. And that was on top of a caseload that was already delivering revenue of $850,000 a year—all because the MGO had the time to focus entirely on her donors. Extra time well spent translated into significant added revenue.

This isn't magic, simply logic—but it's logic that needs to get in front of every manager who is holding back on administrative help. Many nonprofit leaders just do not value support people. One of our professional goals is to categorically show that additional support for an MGO will actually bring in far more revenue than the cost.

But don't wait for us to prove it. Use these logics and arguments to make a case for hiring a support staff. If, after you make the case, the authority figure in your life wants to keep things status quo, then he or she should be happy with lower revenue.

Get Through the Daily Grind

We're not sure if it's actually Buddhist or not, but we love the proverb about the dung beetle: "If we are facing in the right direction, all we have to do is keep on rolling."

We once saw that quote on a cartoon which had a little sign in the background that declared, "Dung profits up 140%!!" We think we could all believe that. There's certainly plenty of manure to be found—even in the major gifts world we live in. Think about it— we all have to deal with:

- ▶ Hours spent researching donor information.
- ▶ Managers who don't think we need support.
- ▶ Demands for increased revenue production.
- ▶ Donors who are angry or frustrated.
- ▶ Voices in our heads telling us we're not going to make it.
- ▶ Meetings that have very little to do with our caseload.
- ▶ Office politics and bureaucracy.
- ▶ Systems that don't work.
- ▶ Program-funding surprises.
- ▶ People who believe that MGOs do nothing but run around and have fun.
- ▶ Donors who don't answer the phone or e-mails.
- ▶ Donors who change their minds.

It's Not Just About the Money

The list could go on, if we were to try to mention everything tedious, tiring, or challenging about our work. And many MGOs actually do focus on that—as do their managers. They spend their entire lives focusing on the negative. It's no wonder they don't succeed.

The fact is that in any human endeavor most of the effort is more about plodding through than maintaining a constant high. So instead of focusing on what's wrong, remember that it really does take a great deal of effort and energy to get things right and achieve success. Unfortunately, it means you sometimes have to focus on the things you know you must do to find your pace in your major gifts work-things like:

- ✔ Getting in touch with donors to qualify them. One MGO we know recently sent us an e-mail saying, "In 30 days, I stopped by the homes or businesses of 171 donors, had 42 terrific face-to-face donor visits, and discovered a wealth of information about many of those I didn't get a chance to speak with. It was an exhausting but very fruitful month!"
- ✔ Following on from the example above ... learning more about donors, their lives and interests. The more you know, the more prepared you are to present to them an opportunity they want to support!
- ✔ Spending hours trying to get in touch with donors, then, instead of talking, stopping to listen, with a compassionate ear and heart, to their concerns and problems.
- ✔ Missing revenue projections and feeling anxious about it while you develop an alternate plan.
- ✔ Waiting for program folks to get you information for an ask or to report back.
- ✔ Writing, and writing, and writing when you could be out of the office.
- ✔ Having to deal with management and team members who seem unsupportive or indifferent.

- ✔ Constantly looking at your contact priorities to make sure you're talking to the right ones, not just those you like the most.
- ✔ Traveling great distances and working during off hours.

But you have to do all this work to be successful. Money will not just drop into your hands. You know that. And that's why you must persevere through the grueling day-to-day of your major gifts work. It's a tough job that takes perseverance, which is a continued effort to do or achieve something despite difficulties, failure, or opposition.

So what are we saying? Life is tough? Yeah. Accept the fact that many of your workdays will be grueling and intense. And that's OK, as long as you remember to embrace those grueling days, difficulties, failures, rejection, opposition and tedious work. Don't run from them! Don't devalue them! Embrace them as a very real and human part of being successful in major gifts. Aiming only for really good and easy days often gets you nothing very great.

And if you do this, you will be acknowledging the truth that most of your work will not be high-excitement, high-energy, high-pay- off, or high-recognition. This adjustment in your attitude and work philosophy will reframe your days and your view of life. With this new mindset, you can adopt a work style of perseverance—of working through the tedious and boring to get to your objective. You know you're facing the right direction. Now, just keep rolling.

Meet Expectations

One of the most irritating realities of life is having to deal with the expectations of others. And then, if we're being honest, we have possibly even bigger expectations of others as well—and we get irritated when they don't meet our expectations.

People outside of ourselves have expectations and we have expectations for everyone around us. Seems normal, doesn't it? Then why do we get so irritated about it? Most likely it's because

It's Not Just About the Money

we don't clearly understand the value of the expectations others had for us. And because we don't understand, the expectations feel unreasonable and bothersome. This dynamic repeats itself over and over again in major gifts. There are some basic expectations in the major gift world. Here are the most common ones:

- ✔ **Donors expect to be thanked.** We all know what it feels like to do something nice for someone and not be thanked, so take a moment this week to map out the thank-you process in your organization. Put it on a PERT chart and write down the steps and amount of time it takes. Does it feel right to you? Then, try sending yourself the thank-you letter you send to a donor. Does it make you feel appreciated? It's always good to check your thank-you system at the beginning of each year.

- ✔ **Donors expect to be told the truth.** Unfortunately, covering up the truth or even shading it is something that happens too often. Let's say a program isn't going well but the MGO is encouraged to get the funding for it anyway. Or a program is likely to be closed down and the funding continues. Misleading scenarios like those can destroy a donor relationship. Donors can usually handle the truth, but deception hurts.

- ✔ **Donors expect to hear a full response to their questions and concerns.** Have you ever had a situation where a donor asks a tough question or criticizes what you're doing and you just want to shut down? It's a normal reaction. But answer the question. And if you don't know the answer, then say you don't. There's nothing wrong with that. Donors are partners, so they deserve to have their questions answered.

- ✔ **Program people expect their plans to be represented honestly.** Good program people are technicians, creative folks who take pride in how they've constructed a program that will actually help people or the environment or whatever cause their organizations champion. They've spent a great deal of time working up a system, and they know it works. It has a lot of detail and logic to it, and every single part is important. If, as an MGO you minimize the importance of what they do or, possibly worse, embellish it, you are not only stretching the truth, you are diminishing the program person's value. They expect you to truthfully represent what they've created and are managing. You should therefore spend a lot of time getting to know each program of your organization.

✔ **Finance expects the MGO to represent the financial situation fully and correctly.** Finance people are often the most misunderstood people in a nonprofit. We call them bean counters and often try to make them small through our comments and attitudes, and that's because we don't understand them. In fact, if we didn't have them in our lives and work, things would be in shambles. Finance folks are a gift to us. They make sure the economics of what we are trying to do in helping others actually works and stays on track. That's why they get fussy when someone doesn't follow protocol and either manages money poorly or represents a financial situation in the wrong way. Two legs of the nonprofit stool are program and fundraising. The third leg is finance.

✔ **Managers expect performance—meaning revenue.** (You knew this one was coming, didn't you?) We find it really fascinating that an MGO could take a job knowing that the main responsibility is to raise money, but then resent the manager who expects her to raise that money. Or that an MGO can get annoyed that her manager is "clipping her wings" by asking her to focus exclusively on her caseload and not other activities.

Expectations are all around us, from the donor to program, finance to management. If you think about it, most of their expectations are reasonable, even helpful. So when you feel burdened by them, turn and embrace them, as they can make you better at your job. Just as important, they'll make your work more effective.

Pursue Management Values

Think of two managers in your career—one whom you loved and one you didn't. (You might be reporting to one or the other as you read this.) The managers we don't like usually are those who misused their power. There's a Greek Proverb: "The measure of a leader is how he or she uses power." Remember this: Power misused is symptomatic of an insecure person who doesn't know what to do. We should feel sorry for such people rather than getting angry. But they can be so frustrating!

Yet our anger isn't only reserved for managers who misuse their power. MGOs get upset with management for simply pursing the organization's values. We know an MGO who got so upset about "the demands of management" that he ended up alienating his manager, getting his focus off of his caseload, failing at his job, and, finally, getting fired.

Strangely, this happened because his manager, who is very good, simply wanted this MGO to pay attention to some basic things that were important to the organization. Understand that most managers are reasonable and that the values they pursue are worth your attention and support. Let's look at what good management tends to value:

1. **A caseload with predictable economic value.** This is about ratios and return on investment. It's totally reasonable for management to expect a certain return on the money it spends toward the major gifts effort. That return ultimately needs to be better than direct mail and events, so a good manager will be looking for the organization to receive $3 or $4 for every dollar the organization spends on you and your work.

If you add up all the costs of your job, including your salary, benefits, support, operating costs and expenses, multiply that times three for new major gift programs, times four or five for programs in their second and third year, and up to six and higher for older major gift programs, you should reach an ambitious but reasonable revenue target.

We have clients with returns of from 1:6 to as high as 1:20. Consistently. If the revenue return of your effort is low, it will seriously affect the fundraising ratios of the organization, a value that it's very important to guard— which is precisely why management worries about it. But it's not solely about the ratios. It's about securing as much money for major gift programs as possible while satisfying the passion and interests of your donors.

2. A healthy share of undesignated gifts. Management wants flexibility and to be able to cover every cost. If all an MGO does is secure designated gifts, his job could be in trouble. Why? Because it takes undesignated gifts to cover his salary.

Programs, by their very nature, are changing due to the environment and circumstances of the people they reach. Outfitting the math classroom of Mr. Jones in the Fairfield Elementary School of Corning, NY, is substantially more specific than supporting math education in Corning. At the beginning of the school year the program people planned to outfit that specific classroom, as the year wore on it turned out that state funds came in to cover the cost. So where would you be if you'd secured the money from a donor in this case? You'd have to give it back or go to the donor and politely ask if he'd give it to something else. Not an easy task.

Designated money is often easier to secure, but it's most often harder to manage. That's why managers want more undesignated money than designated. One word about donors on this point: It is important to disclose this dynamic to the donor. When you do, most of them understand. Sure, they enjoy supporting a specific project, but they will also recognize the need for the organization to place funding where it's needed most, rather than into a program with little flexibility.

3. The inclusion of overhead with direct program costs. Overhead, before all the allocations take place, often runs at

20 percent to 30 percent of total spending. As we mentioned elsewhere, some think it should be 8 percent to 15 percent. It's not. But nonprofits have backed themselves into a corner here by effectively selling the donating public on the myth that a nonprofit can run on practically nothing. (That's another chapter.) The main point here is that overhead is significant and management needs to make sure all the costs are covered.

Organizations should take overhead costs and spread them proportionately across the programs. So, if the direct costs to dig 500 wells in Tanzania is $300,000, and that amount represents 10 percent of the total program budget for that year, then the program should carry 10 percent of the total overhead. Say the total program budget of this organization is $3 million. The overhead is $750,000, making the total budget $3.75 million. So a $300,000 program should carry $75,000 in overhead, which means that if a donor wants to fund the whole thing, the cost will be $375,000, not $300,00.

Not many people think this is a good idea, feeling that they couldn't in good faith add that kind of money to program costs. We don't know where we got the idea that running programs is only about the direct costs. Or that charging program with overhead costs is a moral issue. It's crazy, because where is the rest of the money supposed to come from? It's impossible to run a nonprofit without overhead, which is why management wants overhead covered.

4. Being frequently in touch, but not often in the office. You can't be connecting with donors if you're sitting at your desk, unless you're writing them letters, sending e-mails or talking to them on the phone. But if you're there most of the time, you can't be having any face-to- face contact, which is very important. If you're an MGO and doing your job while sitting at your desk, be sure to communicate up-line that, in fact, you are connecting with your donors.

5. Generosity with credit for major donations. Most of you have experienced this: You should get credit for a gift from a donor on your caseload and, surprise, credit goes to someone else—the planned-giving person, the foundations role, you name it. On one hand, you need the credit to show that you're doing your job. On the other, management wants a team player who isn't always obsessed with what she achieves. Maybe you can get soft credit and the other person puts the number on his books. Just move on. It'll play better with management and remind them you know you are doing your job. If on the other hand, you keep pressing and pressing, it can seem desperate and insensitive. You might win a battle without scoring any points.

6. Working as a happy team, not competitive individuals. Like the previous principle, this goes beyond caseload and credit. If you are unified, caring, flexible, and working as a team rather than as competitors, people notice and they start to become really impressed. If a young, new MGO comes in and you move donors to her, management sees it as an effective team that is ultimately self-managing. The staff member who joined the team but had fewer technical skills is more valuable than the employee with great skill but a rotten attitude. No manger likes a prima donna.

7. Managing expenses wisely and conservatively. This almost goes without saying. But there are still MGOs who spend, spend, spend. Really, it's forgetting to be respectful with cash a donor ultimately gave, and it can't possibly play well with management.

Management consultant and author Peter Drucker once said, "Management is doing things right; leadership is doing the right things." And doing things right means paying attention to the details.

Be OK With Being Alone

Right now, just take two minutes and really consider how your day is going so far. If for some reason you're feeling miserable, that fact may be pretty easy to admit. But anything slightly better than that, right up to almost perfect, is a little harder. For instance, are you happy and fulfilled in your work—successful and at the top of your game? Are things clicking into place for you in a way that finds you saying, "What a great day! I can't believe I have such a great life."

Do you feel supported and valued? Do others at work really care about you? Are they interested in what you do and how you're doing? If you answered yes to all of these questions, things are looking pretty good for you.

Now take a longer view—at your week, your month, the last year. Assuming you're not reading this book aloud to someone, no one will know how you answer, so you can be really honest in your evaluation. Try it, because very few people can actually admit that things are not going as well as they like—the simple reason being that if they admitted it, they would feel like they had to do something about it. And what exactly can they do?

If this were you, would you have to tell someone else that your world is not as rosy as you often present it? Would you feel embarrassed to expose the gap between the perception you create among co-workers, friends and loved ones, and your somewhat less satisfying private reality? Part of this comes from the convention of always answering the question, "How are you?" with the words, "Great, thanks," even when we're not feeling so great. Try being a little more honest and see how quickly the subject changes. Perhaps it's not because people don't want to know, but they just aren't prepared time-wise to find out what's really going on.

You often see the happy front on salespeople, the really friendly types. Richard relates an encounter he had at a recent conference: "I recently met someone at a conference and received a pumping handshake, slap on the back, brilliant smile, raucous laughter. Everything was great. He had enough energy to light a small city. What an incredible world this man seemed to live in. Later that evening, I saw him in the bar alone having a drink, and he looked uncomfortable. In reality, it was just him and his thoughts—and that's true for all of us, so it's best to be in the right place. I felt sorry for him, but it wasn't because he was alone. Not at all. It was because he was alone and uncomfortable being that way. He had no idea that it's actually OK to be solo."

For you as a major gifts officer, development director or manager of a major gifts program, one of the Boring Indispensables is to enjoy being alone. If you can grow to be comfortable with that reality, it will help make your work experience better. If every single day were filled with the arrival of large donations, helpful colleagues who find your work fascinating, happy donors and a manager who thinks you walk on water, everything would be great. Unfortunately, most days aren't like that. Most of your professional and personal life is going to have certain challenges.

So don't buy into the fake reality we see in the media, presenting normal life as constant laughs and euphoria. For an MGO especially, there are long hours alone preparing to speak to donors. Hours on the phone or e-mail trying to get through to them. Long flights and drives alone to meet with donors, only to be stood up, turned down or lectured. There are those long and solitary hours back in the office where at times, you wonder if it all really matters. But here's the good news:

- ✔ We are all in the same boat. Is there comfort in knowing other people feel the same way? Perhaps—if you can share the burden and find out how they deal with it too. Don't think for a moment that someone else is fundamentally happier, whatever they may have. Life is not all rosy for anyone.

- ✔ You matter a great deal. Think on your valuable skills and your good heart that truly cares about others. You are responsible for your mission to do a great job, free to show yourself and others how you can shine.

- ✔ Your work matters. You are doing some of the most important work on the planet! You're connecting people who have resources to people who need them desperately. It really doesn't get better than this.

- ✔ Others are better off because of you. Consider this: Without your efforts, many hundreds, possibly thousands of people's lives would be unchanged. Depending on what you do, some would have died without your work. For others, their lives would never have been so rich and fulfilled. Your organization and your donors wouldn't have the benefit of your time, attention, care, talent, effort, hard work.

- ✔ You are changing the world. This is actually the truth. You are changing the world. That's why we love this work and love talking to you about it. You are making a difference. Never forget that.

So, with all this good news, are you going to let the circumstances of life get you down? Yes, occasionally. But you can also embrace the fact that life has its difficulties, that major gifts work is often a solo job, and that managers and team members might not always appreciate you as you wish they would. The fact is that, on the whole, we all are doing quite well. Don't believe it? Learn to focus on the five pieces of "good news" we've listed above. When things start to get you down, stand up and dust off, grab yourself by the collar and say, "Hey, that's just part of the job." Then turn your focus to the donor.

Always Monitor Cost

Jeff can't stomach the topic of costs, and has said, "It doesn't inspire or interest me." Of course, he was half kidding, because he deals very professionally with this important issue. Even if you are equally uninspired by monitoring costs, you still have to work hard at it.

We see so many major gifts teams, from one-person shops to large departments, who get things wrong in the area of costs. From major gifts people in multimillion-dollar nonprofits right down to the charity set up in someone's spare room at home, you can hear nonprofit folks saying, "Look! All I need to do is raise the money. I don't need to be sitting around worrying about administration, books, and budget. Leave me alone, and let me get on with it!"

If you've ever said something along these lines when your manager has asked to open a discussion on budgeting and costs, next time you should actually welcome the opportunity to investigate this area.

The fact is that right now, there are arguments raging in charities of all sizes all around the world about how much a major gifts program should cost. How much should we pay for an MGO? What kind of support should an MGO have? What ROI should we expect from a major gifts program? Finally, when should we add new MGOs to the program?

If you're like Jeff, this isn't your favorite subject, but stay with us: Your job as an MGO, a manager of major gifts, or even as a one-person shop, could depend entirely on how you handle this one subject.

In this world of diminishing financial resources and competition for every dollar, there are some key financial realities you should know about, because they will help you do the following:

- ✔ Manage your caseload better.
- ✔ Manage the major gifts program more effectively whether you are part of a larger team or just one person in a very small charity.
- ✔ Have more compassion for the management's need to secure a better ROI from the major gifts program.
- ✔ Keep your job, and excel at it.

We believe to our core and have consistently said that major gifts is not about the money. It is fundamentally about donors transferring value from themselves to something they care about. So that, in a few words, explains your relationship to your donor.

But there's another key relationship in this equation: the relationship between the major gifts team and the organization. You and your manager do need to be concerned about the cost of raising money from major donors, because:

It's Not Just About the Money

- ✔ It shows respect to donors and the use of their money.
- ✔ It's the right and responsible thing to do.
- ✔ People inside and outside the charity expect it.

If you think major gifts fundraising is just about donors and program, you're wrong. It's also about how we behave internally, what choices we make, what priorities we have, and how we spend our effort, time and money.

Start by trying to get a handle on how much your major gifts program costs, compared to how much it raises. You must pay careful attention, or the return for every dollar spent can be way below where it should be.

A Closing Thought: Don't Try This Without Passion

Passion has a price. That price is the inability to accept the status quo, or just go with the flow. For a person of passion, mediocrity is the enemy and that's quite a heavy burden.

We talk a lot about how we need to have passion for life and work but, in reality, people with passion are frankly thought of as odd or different in our society. There's so much temptation just to keep your head down, do your job and carry on. In fact, that's the way most of the world works.

As we finish this book, we're going to say something that we hope won't irk you. To be a great fundraiser you have to be passionate not only about your organization's mission, but about fundraising. Some are passionate about one and not the other, but we've never known a truly great fundraiser who isn't passionate about both.

What's incredibly sad is that we've met far too many fundraisers who aren't passionate about either!

Fundraising is hard work. It's draining. It takes all of your effort. And when you make a mistake it could be disastrous. That means it's stressful, which is why if you're not passionate about it, you'll burn out quickly and make yourself miserable. And have we ever encountered many miserable fundraisers in our day! Do you know any?

Honestly and truly, they should leave and find their passion elsewhere, but they've lost even the inspiration to pursue what they love. So they sit in tiny cubicles of fear, worry, pressure, and sometimes sadness and bitterness. They mistreat donors, argue with program people, and figure out ways to get by without having to do too much. We won't ask you to tell us if you've seen this happen, but if you're one of them, make a change. Do it for your own sake and for whatever part of you that knows things could be different, or better.

If you see it in someone else, don't get angry. You should respond with compassion, because these are good, well-meaning and often highly talented people who just haven't found their life's work. Fundraising can be exasperating for the intelligent and gifted person who's simply cut out to expend his or her energies elsewhere.

Now, if you're passionate about fundraising, smile about it. Pressure is high, and passion has a price. But you know the joy of helping people give away their money and the excitement when you connect a donor's values with your organization's work. You've seen a donor with the look that says, "I know I'm receiving more than I gave!" You are aware of that awesome moment when the mystic gulf between the generous giver and the grateful recipient is finally bridged. There truly is nothing like it.

Let us encourage you to live and work from your passion, whether that's in fundraising or not. Open yourself up to the joy to be found and say, "Yes!"

Thank You

This book would not have been possible without the work and support of many people. Jeff and I especially want to thank John McWhinney for making sense of it all, Margaret Battistelli for helping the book take form, Doug Davidson for putting it all together, Ellen Osborne for making it look good, Jeff Brooks for his wisdom, and Lindsay Groff for keeping everyone accountable to get it done—a value we hold very highly.

We also want to thank all those who work and walk with us at Veritus Group: Amy, Ashley, Carter, David, Debi, Diana, Edie, Heidi, Jennifer, Karen, Keturah, Lisa, Lori, Louise, Rebecca, Robert, Samara, Sian, Stephen, Suzanne, Theresa, and Zack. You all are an amazing group of people dedicated to making the world a better place.

And we could not have done this without our families who have journeyed with us for so many years, through long work trips and late nights, through tough times, and great moments of joy. All of those experiences are reflected in this book.

And finally, to all the Major Gift Officers and donors who are embedded in great causes around the world and who, through their wisdom, hard work, thoughtfulness, and generosity are changing lives every day, including ours—we thank you.

About the Authors

Richard has more than 40 years of nonprofit leadership and fundraising experience. He was a Development Director of a major international relief and development organization and a cofounder of The Domain Group, which became one of the largest direct marketing agencies serving non-profits in the United States, Canada, and Europe. Richard, a deeply caring counselor who helps donors fulfill their passions and interests, believes that successful major gift fundraising is not fundamentally about securing revenue for good causes. Instead, it is about helping donors express who they are through their giving. Richard is the founding partner of Veritus Group.

Jeff has over 32 years' experience in nonprofit fundraising, including early work as the Director of Development for two nonprofits. Later, at The Domain Group, Jeff led a team that executed strategic plans and direct-response marketing for clients such as: Feeding America, Arthritis Foundation, American Cancer Society, and the Salvation Army. Armed with knowledge and passion for fundraising, Jeff joined Richard Perry to form Veritus Group. Jeff and Richard co-author the popular fundraising blog focusing on major gifts called, "Passionate Giving," and a podcast called "Nothing But Major Gifts" as well as numerous white papers all promoting mid-level, major, and planned gift fundraising. Jeff is passionate about life, philanthropy, and relationships.

Made in United States
Orlando, FL
06 May 2023